THE MICROWAVE
FISH COOKBOOK

THE MICROWAVE
FISH COOKBOOK

Val Collins

DAVID & CHARLES
Newton Abbot   London   North Pomfret (Vt)

Acknowledgements

I should like to thank Thorn EMI Domestic Appliances Limited for supplying Tricity microwave cookers and equipment for the photography.
Colour photography by John Plimmer, RPM Photographic, Havant.
Line illustrations by Mona Thorogood.
With grateful thanks to Charles Payne—a keen angler—who gave me the idea for this book, and to Jayne Cundy for her assistance with the preparation of food for photography.

British Library Cataloguing in Publication Data

Collins, Val
   The microwave fish cookbook.
   1. Cookery (Fish)
   I. Title
   641.6′92   TX747

   ISBN 0-7153-8393-0

Phototypeset by ABM Typographics Limited, Hull
and printed in The Netherlands
by Smeets Offset BV, Weert
for David & Charles (Publishers) Limited
Brunel House   Newton Abbot   Devon

Published in the United States of America
by David & Charles Inc
North Pomfret   Vermont 05053   USA

Contents

Introduction

As an enthusiastic user of the microwave cooker, I agreed whole-heartedly when a keen angler once said to me that, in his opinion, fish cooked by microwave was the best he had ever tasted. I was delighted to hear this as it seemed to me that it must be so if someone who is used to eating freshly caught fish can also remark upon the perfect results obtained from the microwave cooker. Probably more than all other foods, fish benefits from being cooked by microwave as the moist texture and delicate flavour is preserved and to a degree even enhanced by this cooking method.

With its speed of cooking and the fact that little or no additional liquid is required, the microwave cooker ensures a delicious result while retaining more vitamins and minerals than most other cooking methods—and, of course, there is the additional advantage of savings on energy consumption. With no oven to pre-heat and a reduction of up to 70 per cent on normal cooking times—depending on what you cook—the microwave cooker can cut your cooking fuel bills by as much as half.

In the past, it was probably only people who lived on the coast who took full advantage of the fish readily available to them. But in these days of refrigerated transportation, a plentiful daily supply of fresh fish is available to us all in the shops. A good fishmonger is only too willing to advise and assist on the selection, cleaning and preparation of the fish and, given a few days' notice, he will obtain a special order of a less popular type if it is in season.

Whatever fish you choose—a delicate white fish, a richer oily fish or one of the delicious varieties of shellfish—all provide us with an excellent source of protein to supplement and add variety to our diet, whether served as a starter, a main course, or a light luncheon or supper dish.

Generally, the British taste in fish dishes is plain and fairly simple, but interest in more exciting recipes has increased thanks to worldwide travel. More elaborate dishes with delicious sauces and an exciting combination of different fish are available and I have included in this book a selection of my favourites for you to try. I am sure that you, your family and friends will be delighted with the results.

The microwave cooker

Before beginning to use the microwave cooker, it is important to know how it operates and to read and understand all the facts given in the manufacturer's user instructions. This provides specific information for your particular model and, together perhaps with a reputable book on basic microwave cooking, will give explicit detail about the behaviour of microwave energy and on the operation and care of the appliance.

The design of microwave cookers varies between the different manufacturers' models, but they all have a similar appearance and the basic principles of microwave cooking remain the same, although new and recent developments have made a wide choice of models available.

Standard units with on/off controls have been introduced with additional features such as defrost controls, selector or variable power controls, turntables, browning elements and temperature probes. The control panel on a microwave cooker consists mainly of one or two timers, a defrost control and/or variable power control, indicator lights and a start or cook button. There are now available some models with sophisticated electronic programming and sensing devices, and touch control systems. With no knobs, dials or

Fish Plaki (page 22)

switches, the cooker is operated by simply touching the appropriate section of the control panel.

The timer control is most important—as microwave cooking is gauged by time, not time and temperature—and is marked so that the shorter heating or cooking periods can be set with a degree of accuracy.

The variable power or selector control gives a greater flexibility and control of the cooking speed, which may be compared with the equivalent of conventional oven settings. With many food items this is unnecessary, but can be invaluable for those foods or dishes which may benefit from longer, slower cooking. There are two methods used by manufacturers to vary the power into the oven. Either the microwave energy is cycled on and off at varying rates depending on the setting chosen, or the power into the oven is altered to provide continuous but lower speed cooking.

Different manufacturers portray the variable power settings on the control panels of their models in different ways. It is useful to compare these in chart form to enable you to adapt the cooking times given in this book to suit your particular model, but do check your microwave cooker instructions with reference to the description of settings related to the percentage and power inputs.

1 Keep Warm LOW 150W 25%	2 Simmer DEFROST 200W 30%	3 Stew MEDIUM-LOW 250W 40%	4 Defrost MEDIUM 300W 50%	5 Bake MEDIUM-HIGH 400W 60%	6 Roast HIGH 500W 75%	7 High FULL 650W 100%

By using the chart given below, it is possible to adapt the cooking times given in this book to suit your own particular model. However, the timings given in the chart are intended as a guide only, as much depends on the shape, density, texture and temperature of the food. The calculations have been based on a microwave cooker with an average power output of 650 watts and, of course, this may vary between different models. Allow slightly more time if using a microwave cooker with a lower output and slightly less time if using a cooker with a higher output.

Power levels

		10%	20%	30%	40%	50% (defrost)	60%	70%	80%	90%	100% (full)
	1	10	5	3¼	2½	2	1¾	1½	1¼	1	1
	2	20	10	7	5	4	3¼	2¾	2½	2¼	2
	3	30	15	10	7½	6	5	4	3¾	3¼	3
Cooking	4	40	20	13	10	8	7	5¼	5	4¾	4
time	5	50	25	17	12	10	8	7	6	5½	5
(minutes)	6	60	30	20	15	12	10	8	7½	6½	6
	7	70	35	23	17	14	12	9¼	8¾	7¾	7
	8	80	40	27	20	16	13	11	10	9	8
	9	90	45	30	22	18	15	12	11	10	9
	10	100	50	33	25	20	16	13	12	11	10

For times greater than 10 min, add together the figures in the appropriate columns.

Microwave cooking techniques

The microwave cook knows that cooking by microwave does not mean that you must learn completely new cooking techniques and, in fact, most of the basic rules still apply. Special points to watch for are given in the various recipes, but a few reminders of the factors which govern successful results may be worthwhile.

Texture

As microwave cooking is so fast, differences in texture will show up more quickly in the end result. A lighter mixture allows microwave energy to penetrate more easily than a heavier one and will cook faster.

Moisture

Moisture, too, can affect cooking times as microwave energy reacts mainly on water molecules. Some of the recipes in this book have been adjusted to use more or less liquid than you are perhaps used to in order to ensure successful results.

Starting temperature

Differences in the temperature of the food when placed into the microwave will affect the length of cooking time required. The colder the food, the longer it will take to cook, so allowances must be made when using food straight from the refrigerator or freezer.

Quantity

As the quantity of food placed in the oven is increased, the length of cooking time also needs to be increased proportionately. Similarly, if you use less than the quantities given in the recipes, the cooking times should be adjusted.

Arrangement of food in the cooker

When heating or cooking a number of similar items together, they should be of even size where possible and arranged in a circle on a plate or on the cooking shelf.

Stirring and turning

Stirring during a heating or cooking process is recommended in some dishes to ensure an even distribution of heat. When it is not possible to stir, particularly when cooking large, whole items, then simply rearrange the dish in the oven cavity by giving it a half or quarter turn. This is not always necessary if a microwave cooker with a turntable is used.

Standing time

All foods continue cooking to a degree when removed from the oven and some dishes will require this standing or resting period to assist with the heating or cooking process. When cooking a flatter dish like a quiche, or a large whole joint of meat, a standing time may be allowed either during or after the cooking process to allow the heat to penetrate from the sides into the relatively cooler centre.

Covering foods

When cooking conventionally, lids on dishes or saucepans assist the food to heat through more quickly; it is the same when cooking in the microwave. Whether a lid on the casserole dish is used or food is covered with clingfilm, the steam is trapped inside and this will enable even and slightly faster results to be obtained. Covering food also allows minimal liquid to be used and ensures no flavour loss.

Utensils

A big advantage of microwave cooking is that foods may be cooked and served in the same dish. Containers are generally easier to clean and food tends not to stick as heat is only produced within the food itself.

Microwave energy is reflected from metal which means that aluminium, aluminium foil, tin, copper and stainless steel containers must not be used. However, microwave energy passes through glass, pottery and china and so, provided that they have no metal trim, these are all excellent containers when cooking in the microwave. Some pottery and china absorb more microwave energy which makes them less efficient. If in doubt, it is worth checking a container by carrying out a simple test. Pour a glass of water into the dish in question and place in the microwave. After $1\frac{1}{2}$ min cooking time the water should be hot and the dish cool. If the reverse is found, then the dish must not be used. On the other hand, if both the dish and the water are warm, then the dish could be used, but as it is absorbing some microwave energy it is less efficient and cooking times would be longer. Most dishes remain cool as microwave energy passes through them to be absorbed by the food, but during cooking there may be some heat transfer from the food to the dish, so be careful when removing them from the cooker.

Suitable containers

To the new microwave user, I normally recommend sorting through the containers and dishes already available before embarking on buying new ones. Quite often it is possible to improvise, and most cupboards have an assortment of suitable ovenproof glass or pottery bowls and pie dishes. Ovenproof glass and pottery flan dishes can be used equally well in the conventional oven or in the microwave cooker for tarts or quiches, and oven-to-table casserole dishes are excellent for microwaves. Roasting bags and boiling bags are ideal for cooking foods such as vegetables as they can be easily shaken or turned over to stir the contents during the cooking. Remember, however, that the wire ties supplied with some makes must not be used. Rubber bands or string ties make suitable alternatives and the bag should be tied loosely to allow some steam to escape. The food will remain hot for a considerable time after cooking if the bag is not opened; it is possible, therefore, to cook several items of food one after another and serve them together.

Shapes and sizes

Generally, the more regular the shape of the container the better it is for even heating or cooking. A round dish is preferable to an oval one and a straight-sided dish better than one which is curved. A container which is slightly rounded at the corners rather than one with square corners will help to prevent food from overcooking at these sharper edges. Larger, shallow dishes are preferable to smaller, deep ones as the greater surface area allows more penetration of the microwave energy; and it is important to ensure that the

Skate with Caper Butter (page 83)

container is large enough to hold the food to be heated or cooked. Light sponge cakes and pudding mixtures in particular rise extremely well to almost double their volume, so remember to only fill the container half full of the uncooked mixture.

Special microwave containers
A wide choice of special microwave cooking containers and dishes is available on the market, but a selection would depend on your needs and preferences. Some of these utensils are intended for conventional as well as microwave cooking, and others are suitable for both microwave and the freezer, which are added advantages.

Browning dishes
These are specially designed for use in the microwave cooker. In appearance they are normal glass ceramic or pyroflam dishes but have a special tin oxide coating on the base. When the dish is pre-heated in the microwave cooker, the base absorbs microwave energy and gets very hot. Food such as steak, chicken portions, sausages, bacon or chops are placed on to the hot base which sears the outside of the food, similar to grilling or frying, while microwave energy cooks the food. Browning dishes can be used for some fish recipes which require a light 'frying' application, for example when cooking fish fingers or fish in breadcrumbs.

Paper
Kitchen paper may be used in the microwave to absorb moisture when reheating or cooking pastry items. The food can be either placed on a layer of kitchen paper, or alternatively a piece may be placed lightly over the top of the dish during the heating period.

Aluminium foil
Small smooth pieces of aluminium foil may be used to cover bones or narrower ends of fish, meat or poultry for part of the heating or cooking time to prevent overcooking. Care should be taken to ensure the foil is smoothed tightly around the ends. By using aluminium foil this way you are, in fact, preventing the microwaves from reaching that area of the food as they are reflected from metal, thus slowing down the heating time. Foil should not be allowed to touch the sides, rear, door or top of the interior.

Preparation and cooking

The cleaning and preparation of fish and shellfish for cooking in the microwave is virtually the same as for cooking by conventional methods and the size and thickness of the fish will affect the cooking times.

Fish which are normally steamed, poached or baked are particularly good. Whole fish, fillets, steaks or cutlets of fish can be cooked without any additional liquid other than perhaps a few drops of lemon juice and/or coated with a little melted butter if preferred. A sprinkling of seasonings or herbs will enhance the flavour and appearance. Alternatively, fish may be poached in liquid, such as wine and cream, if a well-flavoured sauce is required.

Breadcrumbed fish may be dotted or brushed with a little butter before cooking, although the breadcrumbed coating will not become crisp unless a browning dish is used. Deep-fat frying must not be attempted in the microwave cooker as the temperature of the oil or fat cannot be controlled.

The secret of cooking fish and shellfish in the microwave is to watch carefully and test at regular intervals as they can easily overcook. It is best to remove the fish when barely done and then allow a standing period to finish cooking. To ensure even cooking, arrange the thicker portions of the fish near the edge of the dish with the thinner parts towards the centre. When cooking more than one at a time, the tail ends of thin fillets or whole fish may be overlapped or placed head-to-tail to prevent overcooking of these thinner parts. Alternatively, a thin strip of aluminium foil may be wrapped around the head and tail end of whole fish or the thin end of fillets for at least half the cooking period.

For best results, cover containers with a lid or clingfilm; rearrange the fish or turn the dish halfway through the cooking time, although this may not be necessary if you have a microwave cooker with a turntable. Fish will turn from translucent to opaque and will flake easily when cooked; if the centre of the fish is still slightly translucent it will usually finish cooking during a 5–10 min standing period before serving.

From the freezer

The microwave cooker will successfully defrost all fish whether it has been freshly caught and frozen at home or chosen from one of the many commercially frozen varieties available. Some of the larger high street supermarkets now provide a wide selection, from something as simple as coley or whiting fillet to whole salmon or lobster.

It is important to ensure that fish and shellfish are evenly thawed in order to obtain the best results when they are cooked afterwards. Defrosting should be carried out on a 50% (defrost) control or setting, although some manufacturers may recommend a lower 30% setting for some microwave cookers with variable power control. For those models without a defrost control or setting, it is still possible to defrost manually by giving short, 1 min bursts of microwave energy followed by standing periods, repeated until completely thawed.

Defrosting times will depend on the thickness of the fish, for example thin plaice fillets will thaw out more quickly than thick cod cutlets. The frozen fish should be placed in a single layer on a shallow dish or plate and covered with a lid or clingfilm. Fish in boil-in-bags may be defrosted and cooked in the bag placed on a plate or the microwave cooker shelf, but the bag should be cut or slit with a sharp knife to allow some steam to escape.

Frozen fish fillets should be separated as soon as possible during the defrosting process and the thinner tail ends can be folded under or wrapped in small pieces of aluminium foil to prevent them from thawing too quickly and starting to cook. The heads and tails of whole fish may also be wrapped in aluminium foil for approximately half the defrosting period. It may be necessary to turn over thicker steaks, cutlets, whole fish or shellfish halfway through the thawing process.

Fish should be cold when thawed; if it is warm in parts, it has started to cook and it is then preferable to remove it from the microwave cooker and allow it to stand until completely thawed. After defrosting, the fish may be rinsed in cold water to remove any remaining ice crystals, or refrigerated until required.

Prepared, cooked and frozen fish dishes should be defrosted using a 50% (defrost) setting, although a lower setting may be used if preferred. Depending on the type of dish, it is sometimes necessary to reheat gently, using a 70% setting, rather than heat too quickly on full power. This is particularly important to ensure that sauces do not overheat before the main fish ingredient has a chance to heat through. As when cooking, the dish should be covered during reheating and allowed to stand for a few minutes before serving.

Fish defrosting and cooking chart

Fish	Defrosting time 50% (defrost)	Cooking time 100% (full)
bass 450g (1lb)	5–6 min, stand 15 min	5–7 min
bream 900g (2lb)	10 min, stand 20 min 5 min, stand 30 min	10–12 min
cod fillets 450g (1lb)	4–5 min, stand 5 min	4–5 min
cod steaks 450g (1lb)	5 min, stand 5 min	6 min
crab claws 450g (1lb)	5 min, stand 5 min	2–3 min
crab, dressed 100g (4oz)	2 min, stand 10 min	—
haddock fillets 450g (1lb)	4–5 min, stand 5 min	4–5 min
haddock steaks 450g (1lb)	4–5 min, stand 5 min	4–5 min
hake steaks 450g (1lb)	5–6 min, stand 5 min	7 min

Pink Trout in Aspic (page 71)

Fish	Defrosting time 50% (defrost)	Cooking time 100% (full)
kipper, 1	—	1–2 min
kipper fillets, boil-in-bag, 200g (7oz)	3 min, stand 5 min	3 min
lobster in ice 350g (12oz)	10 min, pour off water 6 min, break off ice, stand 15 min	—
mackerel 450g (1lb)	6–8 min, stand 8–10 min	5 min
mussels 450g (1lb)	5 min, stand 5 min	—
plaice fillets 450g (1lb)	4–5 min, stand 5 min	4 min
prawns 450g (1lb)	5 min, stand 5 min	—
salmon steaks 450g (1lb)	5 min, stand 5 min	4–5 min
salmon trout 900g (2lb)	8–10 min, stand 20 min 5 min, stand 30 min	8–10 min
scampi 450g (1lb)	5 min, stand 5 min	2–3 min
sole 450g (1lb)	5–6 min, stand 8–10 min	4 min
trout 450g (1lb)	6–8 min, stand 8–10 min	7 min
fish in sauce 200g (7oz)	3 min, stand 5 min	3–4 min

Browning dish chart
Power level: 100% (full)

Food	Pre-heat	Butter or oil	First side	Second side
4 cod portions in breadcrumbs	4–5 min	1 × 15ml tbsp (1 tbsp) oil	2–3 min	3–4 min
2 cod steaks in batter	4–5 min	1 × 15ml tbsp (1 tbsp) oil	2 min	2–3 min
4 fish cakes	5–6 min	15g (½oz) butter	1½ min	1½ min
6 fish fingers from frozen	5–6 min	brush food with melted butter or oil	2 min	1–2 min

Food	Pre-heat	Butter or oil	First side	Second side
1 plaice fillet in breadcrumbs	4–5 min	1 × 15ml tbsp (1 tbsp) oil	2 min	2 min
oven chips 225g (8oz)	3½–4 min	—	2½–3 min	2½–3 min

Important notes

* All cooking is carried out in the microwave cooker using 100% (full) power unless otherwise stated. Some microwave cooking instructions are given for models with variable power control settings, but it is still possible to cook the dish on models without this facility by referring to the Power Level Chart on page 8 and calculating the time required for cooking on 100% (full) power. The automatic intermittent 'off' periods can be achieved manually by allowing the dish to rest at 1–2 min intervals throughout the cooking duration.

* Metal baking tins or metal-trimmed dishes must not be used in the microwave cooker.

* The recommended cooking times are intended as a guide only as so much depends on the power input to the microwave oven cavity; the shape, material and size of the dish; the temperature of the food at the commencement of cooking, and the depth of food in the dish.

* If the quantities of food placed in the cooker are increased or decreased, then the cooking times must be adjusted accordingly.

* Always undercook rather than overcook the food by cooking for a little less time than the recipe recommends, allowing the extra time if required.

* When reheating or cooking foods, best results are obtained if the food is at an even temperature throughout—particularly important when cooking foods after defrosting.

* Some foods, ie casseroles, require stirring during defrosting, reheating or cooking to assist with the heating process. After cooking with microwave energy, heat equalisation or standing time is often recommended. This allows the distribution of heat evenly throughout the food.

* Deep-fat frying must not be attempted as the temperature of the oil or fat cannot be controlled.

* Microwave cooking does not brown some food in the traditional way, but dishes can be finished off in a conventional oven or under a grill if you feel it is necessary.

Recipes

Anchovy

175g (6oz) french beans
2 × 15ml tbsp (2tbsp) salted
  water
225g (8oz) tomatoes, thinly
  sliced
½ cucumber, thinly sliced
salt and freshly ground black
  pepper
1 × 15ml tbsp (1tbsp) chopped
  fresh herbs, eg basil, parsley
1 lemon, grated rind
100g (4oz) canned tuna fish,
  drained
50g (2oz) black olives, stoned
  and chopped
1 clove garlic, crushed
french dressing (page 109)
8 anchovy fillets, halved
  lengthways

Salad niçoise (*serves 4–6*)   *colour page 95*
POWER LEVEL: 100% (FULL)

Serve as a starter to a meal

1 Trim the beans, but leave whole. Wash and place in a bowl or dish with
   the salted water. Cover and cook for 3–4 min, shaking or stirring once
   throughout. The beans should be crisp. Drain and rinse under cold
   running water.
2 Arrange the tomato and cucumber slices in layers in a shallow serving
   dish. Sprinkle with seasoning, herbs and lemon rind.
3 Place small piles of the beans and tuna fish around the centre of the dish
   and scatter the olives over the top. Season again.
4 Beat the garlic into the dressing and spoon over the salad. Arrange the
   anchovy fillets in a lattice style over the top.
5 Leave to stand for 30–40 min before serving to allow the flavours to blend.
   Serve with lemon wedges and brown bread and butter.

DO NOT FREEZE

For serving: lemon wedges and brown bread and butter

50g (2oz) butter
2 large onions, finely sliced
4 large potatoes, cut into very
  thin matchsticks or grated
50g (2oz) can anchovy fillets,
  drained and chopped
pepper and a little salt
150ml (¼pt) single cream
3 × 15ml tbsp (3tbsp) browned
  breadcrumbs

Jansson's temptation (*serves 4*)   *colour opposite*
POWER LEVEL: 100% (FULL) AND 50% (DEFROST)

This traditional Swedish dish makes a substantial lunch or supper meal

1 Melt the butter in a large bowl for 1½ min. Add the onions, toss well in
   the butter, cover and cook for 6 min until transparent.
2 Add the potatoes, stir well, cover and cook for 8–10 min until the
   vegetables are tender.
3 Place half the potatoes and onions in a serving dish and scatter with the
   anchovies. Season with pepper and a little salt.
4 Cover with the remaining potato and onion and press well down into the
   dish. Pour over the cream.
5 Reduce to 50% (defrost) setting, cover and cook for 4–5 min until heated
   through. Sprinkle with browned breadcrumbs and cook, uncovered, for
   2 min. Serve hot.

DO NOT FREEZE

Jansson's Temptation (above);
Herring and Dill Cucumber Salad
(page 46)

25g (1oz) butter
1 large onion, chopped
1 clove garlic, chopped
450g (1lb) potatoes, grated
275ml (½pt) white sauce
    (page 109)
50g (2oz) can anchovies,
    drained and chopped
ground black pepper and a
    little salt
50g (2oz) cheddar cheese,
    grated
25g (1oz) parmesan cheese,
    grated

Anchovy and potato gratin *(serves 4)*
POWER LEVEL: 100% (FULL)

1   Melt the butter in a casserole dish for 1 min. Add the onion and garlic, cover and cook for 5–6 min until tender.
2   Squeeze as much water from the potatoes as possible, add to the dish containing onion and garlic, cover and cook for 8–10 min until tender, stirring twice throughout.
3   Stir in the white sauce, anchovies and seasonings. Wipe down the sides of the dish, and sprinkle with the cheddar and parmesan cheese.
4   Cook, uncovered, for 3–4 min until heated through and the cheese is melted; alternatively, brown under a hot grill.
5   Serve hot, sprinkled with paprika.

For garnish: paprika

2 medium green peppers
50g (2oz) long grain rice
165ml (⅓pt) boiling chicken
    stock
1 onion, peeled and finely
    chopped
salt and freshly ground black
    pepper
1 bay leaf
50g (2oz) can anchovy fillets
2 tomatoes, skinned and
    chopped

Anchovy-stuffed peppers *(serves 2)*
POWER LEVEL: 100% (FULL)

1   Cut a slice from the top of each pepper. Remove the core and seeds. Reserve the slice to use as a lid.
2   Cover and cook the peppers for 2 min, turn them over, cook for a further 2 min.
3   Place the rice in a bowl or dish, stir in the boiling chicken stock, onion, seasoning and bay leaf.
4   Cover and cook for 5 min, stir and cook for a further 3–5 min or until all the stock is absorbed. Remove the bay leaf.
5   Drain the anchovy fillets and rinse in cold water to remove excess oil and salt; chop the fillets finely.
6   Add the anchovy and chopped tomatoes to the rice. Fill the peppers with the rice mixture and replace the lids.
7   Stand the peppers in the serving dish, cover and cook for 3 min. Serve with mixed salad.

For serving: mixed salad

Bass

Casserole of sea bass and rice *(serves 3–4)*
POWER LEVEL: 100% (FULL) AND 70%

1 Place oil, onion and garlic in a bowl. Cover and cook for 3–4 min until the onion is transparent. Add the rice, stir well and cook for a further 1 min.
2 Add half the boiling fish stock or water, cover and cook for 7 min.
3 Place half the rice mixture in a casserole dish and top with the fish. Season to taste with salt and freshly ground black pepper and sprinkle with the herbs. Add the rest of the rice, sufficient fish stock just to cover and the tomatoes; season again.
4 Cover the dish, reduce to a 70% setting and cook for approximately 15 min until the rice is tender, adding more stock if required. Allow to stand for 10 min.
5 Serve hot, garnished with lemon slices.

For garnish: lemon slices

3 × 15ml tbsp (3tbsp) oil
1 medium onion, finely chopped
2 cloves garlic, finely chopped
175g (6oz) long grain rice
425ml (¾pt) boiling fish stock or water, approximately
450g (1lb) fillets of sea bass (or turbot or halibut)
1 × 5ml tsp (1tsp) mixed dried herbs
salt and freshly ground black pepper
small can tomatoes, chopped

Fish korma *(serves 3–4)*   *colour page 115*
POWER LEVEL: 100% (FULL) AND 50% (DEFROST)

This mild fish curry is left to marinate before cooking

1 Prepare and skin the fish and cut the flesh into 2.5cm (1in) cubes. Mix together the turmeric, crushed garlic and 1 carton yoghurt and pour over the fish. Stir and leave to marinate for 1–1½ hr.
2 Melt the butter in a casserole dish for 1 min, add the sliced onion and garlic, cover and cook for 4–5 min until tender.
3 Crush the cloves and cardamom seeds coarsely and add to the onion and garlic. Cover and cook for 2 min.
4 Add the fish, marinade and cinnamon stick to the dish, stir well. Cover and cook on 50% (defrost) setting for 10–12 min, stirring twice throughout. Stir in the remaining yoghurt. Leave to stand for 5 min.
5 Garnish with bay leaves and serve hot with freshly boiled rice.

For garnish: bay leaves
For serving: boiled rice (page 114)

675g (1½lb) sea bass (or cod or haddock)
1 × 5ml tsp (1tsp) turmeric
1 clove garlic, crushed
2 × 150ml (¼pt) cartons natural yoghurt
25g (1oz) butter
1 onion, sliced
1 clove garlic, sliced
5 cloves
5 cardamom seeds
2.5cm (1in) cinnamon stick

Bream

1 sea bream, 900g (2lb),
approximately
5cm (2in) piece fresh root
ginger *or* 1 × 5ml tsp (1tsp)
ground ginger
1 green chilli
2 cloves
2 cardamom seeds
150ml (¼pt) natural yoghurt
1 × 5ml tsp (1tsp) sugar
½ × 5ml tsp (½tsp) salt
25g (1oz) split almonds, toasted

Spiced baked bream *(serves 3–4)*   *colour opposite*
POWER LEVEL: 50% (DEFROST)

This exotic Indian dish uses bream, but almost any large fish may be used. Before cooking, the fish is left to marinade for 1–2 hr

1 Clean the fish, removing skin and head. Wash in cold water and dry. Place in a shallow casserole dish.
2 Mince or chop the root ginger and chilli very finely. Crush the cloves and cardamom seeds coarsely. Mix these together with the yoghurt, sugar and salt. Pour over the fish, making sure it is well coated with the sauce. Allow to marinate for 1–2 hr.
3 Cover and cook for 15–18 min. Allow to stand for 5 min.
4 Arrange the almonds on top of the fish before serving hot with boiled rice.

DO NOT FREEZE

For serving: boiled rice (page 114)

900g (2lb) bream, scaled and
cleaned
salt and freshly ground black
pepper
1 large lemon
2 × 15ml tbsp (2tbsp) olive oil
1 onion, thinly sliced
1–2 cloves garlic, crushed
400g (14oz) can tomatoes
1 × 5ml (1tsp) coriander seeds,
crushed
1–2 × 15ml tbsp (1–2tbsp)
chopped parsley
1 wine glass dry white wine

Fish plaki *(serves 4)*   *colour page 7*
POWER LEVEL: 100% (FULL) AND 50% (DEFROST)

The fish is cooked whole in this Greek-style dish which traditionally includes lemon and tomatoes in the ingredients. This recipe uses bream, but almost any large whole fish is well suited to this cooking method

1 Place the bream in a large casserole dish, sprinkle with salt and freshly ground black pepper and the juice from half the lemon.
2 Put the oil, onion and garlic in a bowl, toss well, cover and cook for 3 min. Stir in the tomatoes, coriander, parsley and wine.
3 Cover and cook for 5–6 min until well blended, stirring twice throughout. Add seasoning to taste, then pour the sauce over the fish.
4 Reduce to 50% (defrost) setting, cover and cook the fish for 12–13 min. Stand for 2 min.
5 Slice the remaining half lemon thinly and arrange on top of the fish. Cover and cook for a further 2–3 min. Allow to stand for 5 min before serving with jacket or boiled potatoes.

For serving: jacket or boiled potatoes

Spiced Plaice (page 86);
Spiced Baked Bream (above)

Brill

675–900g (1½–2lb) fillets of brill (4–6 fillets)
½ lemon, juice and grated rind
salt and pepper
275ml (½pt) white sauce (see method 2)
1 × 15ml tbsp (1tbsp) grated cheese
paprika for sprinkling

Brill with buttered cucumber *(serves 4–6)*   *colour page 85*
POWER LEVEL: 100% (FULL)

The brill is coated in a white sauce and can be served either as a first course or as a light luncheon dish

1 Skin the fish fillets, wash in cold water and dry. Fold the fillets so that the thin ends are tucked underneath and place in a dish. Sprinkle with the lemon juice, rind and seasoning. Cover and cook for 5–6 min.
2 Drain the juices from the fish and use as part of the liquid quantity to make up the white sauce (page 109).
3 Coat the fish with the hot sauce, sprinkle with grated cheese and paprika and cook for 1–2 min to heat through. Alternatively, brown under a hot grill.
4 Arrange the buttered cucumber in the dish with the brill and serve hot.

DO NOT FREEZE THE CUCUMBER

For serving: buttered cucumber (page 113)

675g (1½lb) fillets of brill
15g (½oz) butter
100g (4oz) button mushrooms, sliced
1 wine glass white wine
salt and pepper
1 shallot, finely chopped
275ml (½pt) white sauce (see method 3)
2 × 15ml tbsp (2tbsp) double cream
100g (4oz) peeled prawns

Poached brill with mushrooms and prawns *(serves 4)*
POWER LEVEL: 100% (FULL)

1 Skin the fish fillets, wash in cold water and dry. Cut the fillets in half lengthways.
2 Melt the butter in a shallow dish for 30 sec, add the fish fillets, arranging head-to-tail. Scatter the mushroom slices over the top and pour over the wine. Season lightly, cover and cook for 6–7 min.
3 Drain off the wine and juices and place in a bowl with the shallot. Cook, uncovered, for about 5 min until the shallot is tender and the liquid quantity reduced. Use as part of the liquid quantity to make up the white sauce (page 109).
4 Stir the cream and prawns into the sauce, adjust seasoning, heat for 1–2 min and spoon over the fish and mushrooms.
5 Sprinkle with chopped parsley and serve hot.

For garnish: chopped fresh parsley

Buckling

Buckling pâté *(serves 6)*
POWER LEVEL: 50% (DEFROST)

Smoked mackerel or trout may also be used for this pâté

1 Remove the skin and bones from the buckling, carefully remove the flesh, cut two-thirds of it into large pieces and put the remainder to one side.
2 Beat the seasoning, lemon juice and white wine together and pour over the prepared buckling pieces. Leave to marinate for 2 hr.
3 Mince or pound the white fish with the remaining buckling, stir in the breadcrumbs, egg yolk, butter and cream. Add the marinade from the buckling and mix well together.
4 Layer this mixture with the pieces of buckling in a suitable pâté container —a 15cm (6in) soufflé dish is a good shape or use a small pottery casserole. Start and finish the layers with the white fish mixture. Press down firmly and arrange bay leaves on top. Cover and cook for 7–8 min, allow to stand for 5 min, then cook for a further 4–5 min.
5 Allow to cool. Cover with clingfilm or greaseproof paper and place weights on top of the pâté. Leave in the refrigerator overnight.
6 Uncover and serve from the dish with toast and butter.

For serving: toast and butter

3 smoked buckling
salt and freshly ground black
   pepper
juice ½ lemon
2 × 15ml tbsp (2tbsp) white
   wine
225g (8oz) fresh haddock or
   cod, cooked
50g (2oz) fresh white
   breadcrumbs
1 egg yolk
25g (1oz) butter, melted
1–2 × 15ml tbsp (1–2tbsp)
   double cream
2 bay leaves

Carp

Poached carp *(serves 4)*
POWER LEVEL: 50% (DEFROST)

To remove the slightly muddy smell and taste of the carp, leave to soak for 2–3 hr in salted water before cooking

1 Soak the carp in salted water for 2–3 hr. Remove head and tail, rinse well and dry. Protect the thin ends of the fish by covering with small smooth pieces of aluminium foil.
2 Place the fish in a large casserole dish with the onion, bay leaf, lemon, seasoning and wine. Cover and cook for 18–20 min until the fish flakes easily with a fork. Remove the bay leaf.
3 Serve immediately with melted butter flavoured with a little lemon juice to taste and boiled new potatoes.

For serving: melted butter, lemon juice, boiled new potatoes

1 small whole carp, 1.2kg
   (2½lb) approximately,
   cleaned
1 small onion, finely chopped
1 bay leaf
2 slices lemon
salt and pepper
3 × 15ml tbsp (3tbsp) white
   wine

4 cross-cut pieces of carp, 175g
    (6oz) each, approximately
100g (4oz) button mushrooms
1 × 15ml tbsp (1tbsp) chopped
    parsley
½ small onion, finely chopped
salt and freshly ground black
    pepper
150ml (¼pt) red wine
150ml (¼pt) water
1 × 15ml tbsp (1tbsp) cornflour

Carp with mushrooms *(serves 4)*
POWER LEVEL: 100% (FULL)

The fish is soaked in salted water for 2–3 hr before cooking

1 Soak the fish pieces in salted water for 2–3 hr. Rinse well and wipe dry.
2 Place the fish in a casserole dish and add the rest of the ingredients except the cornflour.
3 Cover and cook for 8–10 min, turning the dish once halfway through.
4 Remove the fish, place in a serving dish, and spoon the mushroom mixture over it, using a draining spoon.
5 Measure 275ml (½pt) of the cooking liquid into a jug. Blend the cornflour with a little of the sauce and stir into the jug. Cook for 1–2 min until thickened, stirring once halfway through.
6 Adjust seasoning and spoon over the fish and mushrooms. Serve hot.

Cockles

3 × 15ml tbsp (3tbsp) oil
1 onion, chopped
1 clove garlic, chopped
450g (1lb) tomatoes, skinned, deseeded and chopped
1 × 15ml tbsp (1tbsp) chopped
    parsley
salt and freshly ground black
    pepper
550ml (1pt) fresh shelled
    cockles
350–450g (12-16oz) noodles,
    freshly cooked (page 114)

Cockles with noodles *(serves 4)*
POWER LEVEL: 100% (FULL)

1 Put the oil into a large bowl with the onion and garlic. Cover and cook for 4–5 min.
2 Add tomatoes, parsley and seasoning to taste. Cover and cook for 2–3 min. The tomatoes should not be overcooked.
3 Wash the cockles very thoroughly in cold running water. Drain and add to the dish. Stir, cover and cook for 2–3 min until just heated through.
4 Pour the sauce over a bed of noodles and serve hot, garnished with slivers of butter and chopped parsley.

DO NOT FREEZE

For garnish: slivers of butter and chopped parsley (optional)

Cod

3 × 15ml tbsp (3tbsp) lemon
    juice
5 × 15ml tbsp (5tbsp) oil
12 peppercorns
½ × 5ml tsp (½tsp) salt
1 clove garlic, crushed
1 bay leaf
4 cod cutlets, 175g (6oz) each,
    approximately
275ml (½pt) tomato sauce
    (page 112)

Cod portugaise *(serves 4)*
POWER LEVEL: 100% (FULL)

The cod cutlets are marinaded before cooking

1 Make a marinade by mixing together the lemon juice, oil, peppercorns, salt, garlic and bay leaf.
2 Rinse the fish in cold water, dry and place in the marinade and leave for 1 hr.
3 Drain the cod cutlets and place them in a shallow dish, cover and cook for 5–6 min. Allow to stand for 2 min.
4 Heat the tomato sauce for about 3 min if necessary, pour the hot sauce over the fish, cover and cook for 2–3 min.
5 Serve hot, sprinkled with chopped fresh parsley.

For garnish: chopped fresh parsley

Cod with Aïoli (page 30)

1 leek, washed and trimmed
40g (1½oz) butter
50g (2oz) white breadcrumbs
40g (1½oz) cheddar cheese, grated
salt and pepper
326g (11½oz) can sweetcorn
2 tomatoes, skinned
1 egg, beaten
4 cod steaks, weighing about 175g (6oz) each

Cod steaks with leek and corn stuffing *(serves 4)*   *colour page 41*
POWER LEVEL: 100% (FULL)

1 Slice the leek and place in a bowl with the butter. Cover with clingfilm and cook for 3 min, stirring once halfway through.
2 Add the breadcrumbs, cheese, seasoning and sweetcorn to the leeks, reserving 2 × 15ml tbsp (2tbsp) of sweetcorn for garnish.
3 Chop one of the tomatoes and add it to the mixture. Bind the stuffing with the beaten egg.
4 Wash and trim the fish. Place in a large casserole and season lightly. Cover and cook for 5 min, then stand for 5 min.
5 Fill the cavity and cover the end of each steak with the stuffing.
6 Slice the remaining tomato and place one slice on each steak. Sprinkle on the reserved sweetcorn.
7 Cover and cook for 3 min, turn and cook for a further 3 min. Serve immediately.

450g (1lb) cod's roe
1 × 15ml tbsp (1tbsp) seasoned flour
2 × 15ml tbsp (2tbsp) oil
freshly ground black pepper

Sauté cod's roe *(serves 4)*   *colour opposite*
POWER LEVEL: 100% (FULL)

The cod's roe slices are lightly fried in a browning dish

1 Cut the cod's roe into 2.5cm (1in) thick slices and dip into the seasoned flour.
2 Pre-heat the browning dish for 6–8 min, add the oil and heat for a further minute.
3 Lay the slices of cod's roe on the base of the dish, pressing down well with a heatproof spatula. Cover and cook for 1 min.
4 Turn the slices over, press down well again, cover and cook for 2–3 min.
5 Serve immediately, sprinkled with freshly ground black pepper. Garnish with lemon wedges and serve with hot buttered toast.

For garnish: lemon wedges
For serving: hot buttered toast

---

1 × 15ml tbsp (1tbsp) oil
1 medium onion, finely chopped
1–2 cloves garlic, finely chopped
4 tomatoes, skinned and sliced
salt and freshly ground black pepper
1 × 5ml tsp (1tsp) dried basil
450g (1lb) fresh cod fillet
150ml (¼pt) double cream

Cod provençale *(serves 4)*
POWER LEVEL: 100% (FULL)

1 Place the oil in a dish, stir in the onion and garlic, cover and cook for 3–4 min until the onion is tender.
2 Add the tomatoes, seasoning, basil and fish and mix carefully together. Cover and cook for 4–5 min.
3 Pour over the cream, stir into the mixture carefully, cover and heat for 1 min.
4 Serve hot, sprinkled with chopped parsley.

For garnish: 2 × 15ml tbsp (2tbsp) chopped fresh parsley

Sauté Cod's Roe (above);
Smoked Cod's Roe Pâté (page 31)

25g (1oz) butter
1.2kg (2½lb) fresh cod, cut
    from the centre of the whole
    fish
salt and pepper
few drops lemon juice

Cod with aïoli (serves 4–5)   colour page 27
POWER LEVEL: 70%

Makes a substantial lunch or supper dish when served with plenty of fresh vegetables

1 Melt the butter in a large casserole dish for 1 min.
2 Rinse the cod in cold water, dry and place in the dish, skin side upper-most. Brush with the melted butter and sprinkle with salt, pepper and lemon juice. Protect the 2 cut ends of the fish with small smooth pieces of aluminium foil.
3 Cover and cook for 15 min; baste with butter and juices and remove pieces of foil. Turn the dish in the microwave cooker and continue to cook, covered, for a further 5 min. Allow to stand for 10 min.
4 Drain the cod and place on a large serving platter. Arrange the vegetables in groups around the edge of the dish and garnish with small bunches of parsley sprigs.
5 Serve hot with aïoli, or alternatively melted butter, handed separately.

DO NOT FREEZE THE AÏOLI

For serving: aïoli (page 108) or melted butter, new potatoes in their jackets and fresh vegetables, ie new carrots, courgettes, french beans
For garnish: small bunches parsley sprigs

675g (1½lb) fresh cod
salt for sprinkling
1 × 15ml tbsp (1tbsp) seasoned
    flour
4 × 15ml tbsp (4tbsp) oil
2 small onions, sliced
2 large green peppers, deseeded
    and sliced
539g (1lb 3oz) can tomatoes,
    drained and quartered *or*
450g (1lb) tomatoes, skinned
    and quartered
salt and freshly ground black
    pepper
1 × 15ml tbsp (1tbsp) chopped
    fresh oregano or parsley

Cod romana (serves 4–6)
POWER LEVEL: 100% (FULL)

The fish is lightly pre-fried using a browning dish

1 Remove the skin from the cod, slice the flesh from the bone and cut into 3.75cm (1½in) pieces.
2 Sprinkle the fish with salt and leave for 30 min to draw out some of the moisture. Rinse well in cold water, pat the pieces dry and toss in the seasoned flour.
3 Pre-heat the browning dish for 6–8 min. Add 2 × 15ml tbsp (2tbsp) oil and heat for 1 min. Add the fish, pressing it down against the hot base of the dish for 10-15sec with a heatproof spatula. Turn the pieces over, press down well again, cover and cook for 2 min.
4 Drain well and remove the cod pieces from the dish. Add the remaining 2 × 15ml tbsp (2tbsp) oil to the dish, stir in the onions, cover and cook for 2 min. Add the peppers, cover and cook for 6 min.
5 Add the cod and tomatoes to the vegetables and mix carefully together. Season to taste, cover and cook for 4 min.
6 Serve hot, sprinkled with chopped oregano or parsley.

Smoked cod's roe pâté *(serves 4–6)*   *colour page 29*
POWER LEVEL: 100% (FULL)

225g (8oz) smoked cod's roe,
   soaked overnight
1 cooked potato or slice of bread
1–2 cloves garlic, crushed
juice of ½ lemon
4–6 × 15ml tbsp (4–6tbsp)
   olive oil
salt and freshly ground black
   pepper

Serve as an appetiser or starter

1   Peel the skin from the cod's roe and mash down well. Warm the potato for 15 sec or soak the bread in cold water and squeeze dry. Add to the cod's roe and blend well together with the crushed garlic.
2   Add the lemon juice and olive oil alternately and taste for seasoning before adding salt and pepper.
3   When quite smooth, pile into a dish and garnish with black olives, lemon wedges and parsley sprigs before serving with pitta bread (which may be warmed in the microwave—4 will take about 1½ min).

For garnish: black olives, lemon wedges and parsley sprigs
For serving: pitta bread

Note: *The pâté may be blended in a liquidiser or food processor if preferred, but a little additional lemon juice or oil or cold water will be needed to soften the mixture*

Crab

Crab and rice salad *(serves 4)*
POWER LEVEL: 100% (FULL)

175g (6oz) long grain rice
   (page 114)
1 red pepper
juice of 1 lemon
4 × 15ml tbsp (4tbsp) olive oil
salt and freshly ground black
   pepper
½ clove garlic, crushed *or*
   pinch powdered garlic
150g (5oz) crabmeat, fresh,
   canned or frozen, thawed
75g (3oz) black olives, stoned
50g (2oz) button mushrooms,
   sliced
40g (1½oz) walnuts, roughly
   chopped

This rice salad uses crabmeat, but salmon, tuna or prawns are good alternatives

1   Cook the rice, then rinse under hot water. Drain well, then spread out on a tray and leave to dry and cool slightly in an airy place.
2   Deseed the pepper and cut into strips. Place in a bowl, cover and cook for 2 min. Leave to cool.
3   Whisk together the lemon juice, olive oil, seasoning and garlic for the dressing. While the rice is still slightly warm, add the dressing and adjust seasoning.
4   When the rice is cold, fork in the remaining ingredients and leave to stand for 10 min before serving on a bed of watercress.

DO NOT FREEZE

For serving: watercress

1 × 15ml tbsp (1tbsp) oil
1 onion, finely chopped
1 stick celery, chopped
425ml (¾pt) boiling chicken
  stock
225g (8oz) sweetcorn, canned
  or frozen, thawed
salt and pepper
100g (4oz) crabmeat
150ml (¼pt) milk
3 × 15ml tbsp (3tbsp) single
  cream or top of the milk

Crab and sweetcorn soup (serves 4)   colour page 92
POWER LEVEL: 100% (FULL)

1   Heat the oil in a large bowl for 1–2 min, add the onion and celery, cover and cook for 3 min.
2   Add the chicken stock, sweetcorn and seasonings and cook for 5 min. Add the crabmeat and cook for 2 min.
3   Blend the soup with the milk in a liquidiser or pass through a sieve. Reheat the soup for 2 min.
4   Stir in the cream and serve sprinkled with the flaked almonds.

For serving: 25g (1oz) flaked almonds, toasted

Note: *If preferred, the soup may be served without puréeing. Use 550ml (1pt) boiling chicken stock and omit the milk. Thicken the soup with 2 × 5ml tsp (2tsp) arrowroot mixed with a little water, then stir in the cream or top of the milk. Mix the almonds into the soup before serving*

DO NOT FREEZE

2 medium aubergines
salt for sprinkling
1 × 15ml tbsp (1tbsp) oil
2 medium onions, sliced
1 × 15ml tbsp (1tbsp) tomato
  purée
1 × 5ml tsp (1tsp) dried
  oregano or basil
225g (8oz) crabmeat
2 × 15ml tbsp (2tbsp) fresh
  brown breadcrumbs
2 × 15ml tbsp (2tbsp) grated
  parmesan cheese
2 × 15ml tbsp (2tbsp) grated
  gruyère cheese
4 × 5ml tsp (4tsp) melted butter

Crab-stuffed aubergines (serves 2 or 4)   colour opposite
POWER LEVEL: 100% (FULL)

1   Cut the aubergines in half lengthways, score the flesh with a knife, sprinkle with salt and allow to stand for 30 min. Rinse well and wipe dry.
2   Brush the cut surface with some of the oil, place cut side down on a plate, cover and cook for 8–10 min or until tender.
3   Heat the rest of the oil in a bowl for 1 min, add the onions, cover and cook for 5–6 min until soft. Add the tomato purée, herbs, crabmeat and breadcrumbs. Mix well together.
4   Scoop the flesh from the cooked aubergines and chop finely or mash down with a fork. Add to the bowl with the crab mixture and heat through for 1–2 min.
5   Pile the mixture into the aubergine skins, sprinkle with the mixed grated cheeses and add 1 × 5ml tsp (1tsp) butter to each aubergine half.
6   Heat through for 4–5 min until the cheese is melted. Alternatively, brown the top under a hot grill.
7   Serve hot or cold with a green salad.

DO NOT FREEZE

For serving: green salad

Crab-stuffed Aubergines (above)

40g (1½oz) butter
4–8 large flat mushrooms,
  350–450g (12–16oz)
  approximately
salt and freshly ground black
  pepper
225g (8oz) crabmeat, fresh,
  canned or frozen, thawed
100g (4oz) cheddar cheese,
  grated
paprika for sprinkling

Crab-stuffed mushrooms *(serves 4)*
POWER LEVEL: 100% (FULL)

Serve as a starter

1   Melt the butter on a plate for 1–1½ min. Peel or wipe the mushrooms, arrange on the plate and brush with the melted butter. Sprinkle with salt and pepper.
2   Cover and cook for 3–4 min. Drain well on kitchen paper and place the mushrooms back on the washed plate.
3   Divide the crabmeat between the 4 mushrooms, spread over the top of each one and sprinkle with the grated cheese and paprika.
4   Cook, uncovered, for 2–3 min until the cheese is melted; alternatively brown under a hot grill.
5   Place each mushroom on a round of toast, sprinkle with chopped fresh parsley and serve hot.

For garnish: 2 × 15ml tbsp (2tbsp) chopped fresh parsley
For serving: 4 rounds of toasted bread

15g (½oz) gelatine
75ml (2½fl oz) white wine
275ml (½pt) velouté sauce
  (page 109)
275ml (½pt) mayonnaise
  (page 108)
150ml (¼pt) double cream
450g (1lb) crabmeat, fresh or
  canned

Crab mousse *(serves 8)*
POWER LEVEL: 100% (FULL)

1   Mix the gelatine into the wine. Heat for 45–60 sec and stir well until dissolved. Stir into the velouté sauce with the mayonnaise.
2   Lightly whip the cream and stir into the mixture with the crabmeat. Turn the mousse into 8 individual ramekin dishes or a 17.5cm (7in) soufflé dish.
3   Chill in the refrigerator until set. Garnish with twists of thinly sliced cucumber and sprigs of parsley.
4   Serve chilled with thin slices of brown bread and butter.

For garnish: thinly sliced cucumber and sprigs of parsley
For serving: thin slices brown bread and butter

175g (6oz) shortcrust pastry
  (page 116)
150ml (¼pt) béchamel sauce
  (page 112)
salt and pepper
225g (8oz) crabmeat, fresh or
  frozen, thawed
150g (¼pt) mayonnaise
  (page 108)
few drops lemon juice
2 hard-boiled eggs, chopped
150ml (¼pt) double cream,
  whipped

Crab flan *(serves 6)*
POWER LEVEL: 100% (FULL)

1   Roll out the pastry, line a 20cm (8in) flan dish and bake blind (page 116). Leave to cool.
2   Beat the béchamel sauce and add seasoning. Mix in the crabmeat, mayonnaise, lemon juice and chopped hard-boiled eggs. Finally, fold in the whipped double cream.
3   Pour the mixture into the cooled flan case and smooth the top. Chill until set.
4   Serve cold, garnished with cucumber slices and chopped parsley as a starter to a meal, or as a main course with mixed salad.

For garnish: thinly sliced cucumber and chopped parsley

Note: *Cooked and shelled prawns, scampi, mussels, scallops, lobster, fresh or canned salmon, or a mixture of these, can be used as alternatives to the crabmeat*

DO NOT FREEZE

Crab gratinée diable *(serves 2–4)*   *colour page 118*
POWER LEVEL: 100% (FULL)

1 Melt the butter in a bowl for 1 min. Add the prepared crabmeat, cheese, breadcrumbs, cream and seasonings.
2 Mix thoroughly and carefully spoon back into the cleaned crab shell or into a small bowl.
3 Cook for 2 min, stand for 5 min, turn and cook for a further 2 min.
4 Slice the banana thinly and dip in the lemon juice to prevent slices from browning. Place around the outside edge of the shell or dish and cook for 1 min.
5 Sprinkle with chopped parsley and serve with dry biscuits or fingers of toast.

DO NOT FREEZE

For garnish: 1 × 15ml tbsp (1tbsp) chopped parsley
For serving: dry biscuits or fingers of toast

25g (1oz) butter
1 dressed crab *or* 350g (12oz) canned or frozen crabmeat
25g (1oz) cheese, grated
25g (1oz) fresh white breadcrumbs
1 × 15ml tbsp (1tbsp) single cream or top of the milk
pinch of each: dry mustard and cayenne pepper
dash of anchovy essence
1 firm banana
few drops of lemon juice

Eels

Stewed eels *(serves 4–6)*   *colour page 37*
POWER LEVEL: 100% (FULL) AND 50% (DEFROST)

Ask the fishmonger to skin the eels for you

1 Wash the eels thoroughly and cut into 5cm (2in) lengths. Place in a casserole dish with the hot water. Add the onion and sprinkle with a little salt.
2 Cover the dish and bring to the boil in the microwave on 100% (full) setting, then reduce to 50% (defrost) and simmer for 10–12 min.
3 Blend the butter with the flour and add this in small pieces to the dish, stirring all the time. Cook, uncovered, for 2–3 min, stirring every minute until thickened. The sauce should have the consistency of thick gravy.
4 Stir in the lemon juice and parsley and adjust seasoning to taste with salt and pepper. Serve hot.

900g (2lb) eels, skinned
550ml (1pt) hot water
1 onion, finely chopped
salt and pepper
40g (1½oz) butter, softened
40g (1½oz) flour
few drops lemon juice
2 × 15ml tbsp (2tbsp) chopped parsley

Haddock

Smoked haddock flan (*serves 6*)   *colour opposite*
POWER LEVEL: 100% (FULL) AND 50% (DEFROST)

175g (6oz) shortcrust pastry
 (page 116)
1 medium leek, washed and
 finely sliced
salt and pepper
225g (8oz) smoked haddock,
 cooked
2 hard-boiled eggs, sliced
275ml (½pt) béchamel sauce
 (page 112)
50g (2oz) cheese, finely grated
450g (1lb) creamed potatoes
 (page 113)

1 Roll out the pastry. Line a 20cm (8in) flan dish and bake blind (page 116).
2 Place the leek in a boiling or roasting bag or covered casserole dish with a sprinkling of salt and 2–3 × 15ml tbsp (2–3tbsp) water and cook for 4–5 min. Drain off the water.
3 Flake the fish, discarding any bones or skin, and place in the bottom of the flan case with the leek.
4 Arrange the slices of hard-boiled egg on the top, sprinkle with salt and pepper and cover with the béchamel sauce.
5 Beat half the cheese into the potato and place the mixture in a forcing bag with a large star nozzle. Pipe the potato around the edge and across the middle of the flan.
6 Heat through on 50% (defrost) setting for 9–10 min, turning every 3–4 min.
7 Sprinkle with the remaining cheese and cook for 1–2 min until the cheese is melted. Alternatively, brown under a hot grill.
8 Serve hot, garnished with parsley sprigs.

DO NOT FREEZE

For garnish: parsley sprigs

Haddock bercy (*serves 4–6*)
POWER LEVEL: 100% (FULL)

675g (1½lb) haddock fillets
salt and freshly ground black
 pepper
few drops lemon juice
150ml (¼pt) water
2 tomatoes, skinned
1 shallot, finely chopped
1 wine glass white wine
25g (1oz) butter, softened
15g (½oz) flour
1 × 15ml tbsp (1tbsp) double
 cream
2 × 5ml tsp (2tsp) freshly
 chopped parsley

1 Wash and dry the fish fillets and place head-to-tail in a shallow dish. Sprinkle with salt and freshly ground black pepper and a few drops of lemon juice. Add the water, cover and cook for 7–8 min, turning the dish halfway through. Drain and reserve the liquid.
2 Cut the tomatoes into quarters, remove the seeds and cut the flesh into thin shreds.
3 Place the shallot and wine in a bowl, bring to the boil in the microwave and cook, uncovered, for 4–5 min approximately until the liquid quantity is reduced by half.
4 Blend the butter and flour together and stir into the wine and onion mixture. Add the cooking liquid from the fish and cook for 2–3 min, stirring every minute until thickened. Add the cream, parsley and tomatoes and heat through for 1–1½ min.
5 Place the fish on a hot serving dish and spoon the sauce over.
6 Serve hot, garnished with toasted croûtes of bread.

DO NOT FREEZE

For garnish: toasted croûtes of bread

Stewed Eels (page 35); Halibut in Cider Cream Sauce (page 42); Fisherman's Slaw (page 104); Smoked Haddock Flan (above)

450g (1lb) haddock fillets
25g (1oz) butter
½ lemon, juice and grated rind
100g (4oz) fresh white
    breadcrumbs
5–6 × 15ml tbsp (5–6tbsp) oil
275ml (½pt) tomato sauce
    (page 112)

Haddock and tomato charlotte *(serves 4)*
POWER LEVEL: 100% (FULL)

1 Lightly grease a large round dish or pie dish.
2 Skin the haddock fillets, place in the greased dish and dot with the butter. Sprinkle with the lemon juice and rind, cover and cook for 4–5 min, turning once. Drain the liquid from the fish.
3 Pre-heat a browning dish for 5–6 min.
4 Sprinkle the breadcrumbs with the oil; mix well to ensure that they are coated with the oil.
5 Add the breadcrumbs to the pre-heated browning dish and cook, uncovered, for 1–2 min until lightly browned, stirring every ½ min.
6 Heat the tomato sauce if necessary for 2–3 min and pour on top of the fish. Smooth the top and sprinkle on the breadcrumbs. Cook for 2–3 min until heated through.
7 Serve hot, garnished with tomato slices.

For garnish: tomato slices

500ml (18fl oz) boiling water
pinch of salt
175g (6oz) long grain rice
350g (12oz) smoked haddock
2 hard-boiled eggs
50g (2oz) butter
1 small onion, chopped
salt and pepper

Kedgeree *(serves 6–8)*
POWER LEVEL: 100% (FULL)

Kedgeree is traditionally a breakfast dish, but it also makes a substantial meal for supper

1 Place the boiling water in a large casserole dish. Add the salt and stir in the rice. Cover and cook for 12 min. Leave to stand for 10 min, when all the water should be absorbed; if not, drain the rice.
2 Wash and trim the fish, place in an ovenware dish, cover and cook for 4 min. Flake the fish, discarding the skin and bones.
3 Chop one hard-boiled egg and slice the other. Melt the butter in a large dish for 2 min. Toss the onion in the butter. Cook for 4 min.
4 Add the rice, fish, chopped hard-boiled egg and seasoning. Mix well and warm through for 3–4 min.
5 Garnish with sliced hard-boiled egg and chopped parsley before serving.

DO NOT FREEZE

For garnish: 1 × 15ml tbsp (1tbsp) chopped parsley

450g (1lb) smoked haddock
    fillets
2 × 15ml tbsp (2tbsp) grated
    onion
1 × 15ml tbsp (1tbsp) lemon
    juice
175g (6oz) cream cheese
2–3 × 15ml tbsp (2–3tbsp)
    plain yoghurt or soured
    cream
salt and freshly ground black
    pepper

Smoked haddock pâté *(serves 4–6)*   *colour page 69*
POWER LEVEL: 100% (FULL)

Serve as a starter or part of a buffet menu

1 Skin the fish, cut into small pieces and place in a casserole dish with the onion and lemon juice. Cover and cook for 5 min, stirring once halfway through.
2 Drain the fish well, then blend in a liquidiser or food processor with the onion, cream cheese and yoghurt or soured cream.
3 Season to taste and divide between individual ramekin dishes or a large serving dish. Leave to chill until firm.
4 Garnish with parsley sprigs before serving with lemon wedges and fingers of toast.

For garnish: parsley sprigs
For serving: lemon wedges and fingers of toast

Creamy haddock and sweetcorn *(serves 4)*
POWER LEVEL: 100% (FULL)

450g (1lb) potatoes, creamed
  (page 113), or 1 medium-
  sized packet instant potato
knob of butter
1 × 15ml tbsp (1tbsp) chopped
  parsley
20g (¾oz) butter
20g (¾oz) plain flour
175ml (6fl oz) milk
225g (8oz) haddock, cooked
  and flaked
50g (2oz) frozen sweetcorn
salt and pepper
2 × 15ml tbsp (2tbsp) single
  cream
paprika for sprinkling

Serve as a starter to a meal

1 Cook and mash the potatoes or make up the instant potato. Mix in the knob of butter and the parsley. Using a large rosette pipe, pipe a border of potato onto 4 scallop shells.
2 Place butter, flour and milk in a bowl. Cook for 1 min, beat thoroughly and cook for a further 1 min. Repeat this operation (approximately 3 times) until the sauce thickens.
3 Add the fish and sweetcorn to the sauce and season to taste. Cook for 1 min, stir and cook for a further 1 min. Add the cream, correct the seasoning and spoon the mixture into the scallop shells.
4 Heat the scallops for 4–5 min. Sprinkle with paprika and serve immediately.

DO NOT FREEZE

Haddock with egg *(serves 2)*
POWER LEVEL: 100% (FULL) AND 50% (DEFROST)

2 medium-sized smoked
  haddock
boiling water
2 eggs
butter

This makes a substantial breakfast, lunch or supper dish

1 Rinse the haddock well in cold water and place in a large shallow dish. Cover and cook for 6–8 min, turning each haddock halfway through the cooking time. Leave to stand for a few minutes.
2 Pour boiling water into 2 small individual dishes or cups to the depth of about 2.5cm (1in). Break an egg into each cup and prick the yolks.
3 Reduce the microwave setting to 50% (defrost) and cook the eggs for 1½–2 min, turning the dishes halfway through if necessary. If not quite cooked, allow to stand for 1–2 min, or replace in the microwave and cook for a further 15–30 sec.
4 Drain the haddock and arrange on serving plates or a dish. Lift the eggs from their dishes with a draining spoon and place one on top of each fish.
5 Dot with small knobs of butter and serve immediately.

DO NOT FREEZE

25g (1oz) butter
1 small onion, finely chopped
675g (1½lb) haddock fillets,
    4 pieces weighing
    approximately 175g (6oz)
    each
salt and freshly ground black
    pepper
1 orange, grated rind and juice
25g (1oz) fresh brown
    breadcrumbs
50g (2oz) walnuts, finely
    chopped

Haddock with orange and walnuts (serves 4–6)   *colour opposite*
POWER LEVEL: 100% (FULL)

1   Melt the butter in a casserole dish for 1 min. Add the onion and toss well
    in the butter. Cover and cook for 3 min.
2   Arrange the fish head-to-tail in the dish, season lightly and pour over the
    orange juice.
3   Cover and cook for 6–7 min, turning once halfway through if necessary.
4   Mix together the breadcrumbs, walnuts and grated orange rind, season
    lightly and scatter over the top of the fish.
5   Cook, uncovered, for 1–1½ min. Garnish the dish with orange segments
    and watercress before serving.

DO NOT FREEZE

For garnish: orange segments and watercress

450g (1lb) haddock fillets
salt and pepper
275ml (½pt) béchamel sauce
    (page 112)
100g (4oz) cheese, grated
75g (3oz) peeled shrimps
½ small onion, grated
3 × 15ml tbsp (3tbsp) cream
2 × 15ml tbsp (2tbsp) browned
    breadcrumbs

Haddock in shrimp and cheese sauce (serves 3–4)
POWER LEVEL: 100% (FULL)

1   Wash the haddock fillets and dry. Place head-to-tail in a shallow casserole
    dish and season lightly. Protect thin ends of the fillets with aluminium
    foil if necessary.
2   Cover and cook for 4–5 min, turning the dish halfway through. Allow to
    stand for a few minutes, then drain.
3   Make up the béchamel sauce and stir in 75g (3oz) of the cheese, beating
    well until the cheese is melted. Add the shrimps, onion and cream and
    mix well together.
4   Spoon the sauce over the fish. Mix the remaining 25g (1oz) grated cheese
    with the breadcrumbs and sprinkle over the fish. Sprinkle with paprika
    and reheat, uncovered, for 2–3 min. Alternatively, brown under a hot
    grill.
5   Sprinkle with chopped parsley before serving.

For garnish: paprika and chopped parsley

Hake

275ml (½pt) tomato sauce
    (page 112)
6 hake steaks, 900g (2lb),
    approximately
salt and freshly ground black
    pepper
juice ½ large lemon
1 × 15ml tbsp (1tbsp) oil

Baked hake with tomato sauce (serves 6)
POWER LEVEL: 100% (FULL)

1   Make the tomato sauce.
2   Wipe the steaks and place in a large shallow casserole dish. Sprinkle
    with salt and freshly ground black pepper, the lemon juice and oil.
3   Cover and cook for 8–9 min, turning the dish or rearranging the fish
    halfway through if necessary. Drain off most of the liquid.
4   Pour the tomato sauce into the dish, cover and cook for 1–2 min until
    heated through.
5   Serve hot with sauté potatoes.

For serving: sauté potatoes

*Cod Steaks with Leek and Corn
Stuffing (page 28); Haddock with
Orange and Walnuts (above)*

Halibut

Halibut steaks with fennel sauce *(serves 4)*

POWER LEVEL: 100% (FULL)

4 halibut steaks, 175g (6oz)
    each, approximately
few drops lemon juice
salt and pepper
slivers butter (optional)
275ml (½pt) fennel sauce
    (page 110)

1 Wipe the halibut steaks and place in a shallow dish or on a plate. Sprinkle with a few drops of lemon juice and salt and pepper.
2 Place a few slivers of butter on top of the steaks, cover and cook for 6–7 min. Allow to stand for 3–4 min, then drain off the liquid.
3 Make the fennel sauce and place in a sauce boat or jug. (The sauce can be made in advance and reheated in a suitable container for 1½–2½ min before serving.)
4 Garnish the halibut steaks with parsley sprigs and lemon twists and serve hot with the fennel sauce handed separately.

Halibut steaks with hollandaise sauce

Cook the halibut steaks and garnish as above and serve with freshly made hollandaise sauce (page 109).

For garnish: parsley sprigs and lemon twists

Halibut in cider cream sauce *(serves 4)*   *colour page 37*

POWER LEVEL: 100% (FULL)

4 halibut steaks, 175g (6oz)
    each, approximately
1 medium onion, finely
    chopped
salt and freshly ground black
    pepper
275ml (½pt) dry cider
50g (2oz) mushrooms, finely
    sliced
3 × 5ml tsp (3tsp) cornflour
2 × 5ml tsp (2tsp) water
4 × 15ml tbsp (4tbsp) double
    cream

1 Wipe or wash and dry the fish and place in a casserole dish with the onion, seasoning and cider. Cover and cook for about 7 min, turning the dish once throughout if necessary.
2 Remove the halibut steaks from the dish and keep warm. Return the dish with the cider and onion to the microwave and cook, uncovered, for about 5 min until the liquid quantity is slightly reduced.
3 Add the mushrooms, cover and cook for 2 min. Blend the cornflour with the water, stir into the sauce and cook for 1 min until thickened, stirring once halfway through.
4 Stir in the cream, adjust seasoning and spoon the sauce over the fish. Garnish with a few parsley sprigs before serving hot.

DO NOT FREEZE

For garnish: parsley sprigs

Halibut with mushrooms and tomatoes *(serves 4)*

POWER LEVEL: 100% (FULL) AND 70%

25g (1oz) butter
1 medium onion, sliced
225g (8oz) button mushrooms,
    sliced
400g (14oz) can tomatoes,
    drained and roughly chopped
1 × 5ml tsp (1tsp) dried
    marjoram
salt and freshly ground black
    pepper
4 halibut steaks, 175g (6oz)
    each, approximately
150ml (¼pt) double cream

1 Melt the butter in a casserole dish for 1 min. Stir in the onion, toss well in the butter, cover and cook for 3 min. Add the mushrooms, stir well, cover and cook for 3 min.
2 Stir in the tomatoes, dried marjoram and seasoning. Add the fish steaks, cover and cook for 6–7 min.
3 Stir in the cream, reduce to 70% setting and cook for 1½–2 min until heated through without boiling.

DO NOT FREEZE WITH THE CREAM

Halibut with avocado *(serves 4)*
POWER LEVEL: 100% (FULL)

Turbot or cod steaks may be used as alternatives if preferred

1 Wipe the fish and remove the skin if preferred.
2 Melt the butter in a large shallow casserole dish for 1 min. Add the fish and brush with the butter. Cover and cook for 6 min.
3 Peel and remove the stone from the avocado and mash the flesh well until smooth. Stir in the chopped egg, lemon juice, white wine vinegar and seasoning.
4 Drain the fish and return to the dish. Divide the avocado mixture between the fish steaks and spread evenly.
5 Mix together the breadcrumbs and cheese and sprinkle over the top. Cook, uncovered, for 1½–2 min until heated through and the cheese is melted. Alternatively, brown under a hot grill.
6 Sprinkle with paprika and garnish with lemon twists before serving.

DO NOT FREEZE

For garnish: paprika and lemon twists

4 halibut steaks, 175g (6oz) each, approximately
25g (1oz) butter
1 large ripe avocado
1 hard-boiled egg, chopped
2 × 5ml tsp (2tsp) lemon juice
1 × 15ml tbsp (1tbsp) white wine vinegar
salt and freshly ground black pepper
2 × 15ml tbsp (2tbsp) fresh breadcrumbs, browned
50g (2oz) cheese, grated

Herring

Soft roe savoury *(serves 1–2)*
POWER LEVEL: 100% (FULL)

1 Wash the roe and dry with kitchen paper.
2 Melt the butter in a shallow dish in the microwave for 1 min.
3 Add the roe, cover with a lid or clingfilm and cook for 1½ min.
4 Turn the roe and cook for a further 1 min. Season and garnish with chopped parsley and lemon juice.
5 Serve on hot buttered toast.

DO NOT FREEZE

For serving: slices hot buttered toast

12 soft herring roes, 100g (4oz), approximately
25g (1oz) butter
salt, black pepper
chopped parsley
few drops of lemon juice

Roll mops *(serves 4)*
POWER LEVEL: 100% (FULL)

1 Clean and bone the herrings. Roll up tightly from the tail end. Secure with a wooden cocktail stick if necessary.
2 Place in a shallow dish with the herbs, seasoning and onion. Mix the water and vinegar together and pour over the fish. Cover the dish with a lid or clingfilm.
3 Cook in the microwave for 6–7 min. Allow to cool in the cooking liquor.
4 Serve cold as a starter or with salad.

4 fresh herrings
1 blade mace
1 bay leaf
2 cloves
6 peppercorns
pinch of salt
1 onion, chopped
150ml (¼pt) water
150ml (¼pt) vinegar

50g (2oz) butter
1 medium onion, finely sliced
8 herring fillets
salt and freshly ground black
    pepper
15g (½oz) flour
2 × 5ml tsp (2tsp) french
    mustard
pinch sugar
275ml (½pt) water
75ml (2½fl oz) single cream
25g (1oz) cheese, grated

Herrings in mustard sauce *(serves 4)*
POWER LEVEL: 100% (FULL)

1   Place 40g (1½oz) of the butter in a large shallow dish and melt in the microwave for 1–1½ min.
2   Add the onion slices, cover and cook for 3–4 min until tender. Remove onions from the dish and keep warm.
3   Place the herring fillets head-to-tail in the dish, overlapping the fillets slightly. Season well, cover and cook for 6–8 min, turning the dish halfway through if necessary. When cooked, drain off any liquid, then scatter the cooked onions over the herrings.
4   Melt the remaining 15g (½oz) butter in a bowl for 30 sec, stir in the flour and blend well together with the mustard and sugar. Gradually add the water, cover and cook for 3–4 min until thickened, stirring every minute.
5   Add the cream and half the cheese. Adjust seasoning, stir well and spoon the sauce over the onions and herrings.
6   Sprinkle with the rest of the cheese and cook, uncovered, in the microwave for 1–2 min. Alternatively, brown under a hot grill.

8 herring fillets
salt and freshly ground black
    pepper
1 small onion, finely chopped
juice ½ lemon
2 × 15ml tbsp (2tbsp) chopped
    fresh mixed herbs, ie basil,
    thyme, parsley
150ml (¼pt) fish stock
2 × 5ml tsp (2tsp) cornflour
1 × 15ml tbsp (1tbsp) water
150ml (¼pt) double cream

Herring fillets in cream *(serves 4)*
POWER LEVEL: 100% (FULL)

1   Skin the herring fillets and cut in half lengthways. Place in a large shallow casserole dish. Sprinkle with seasoning, cover and cook for 5 min. Leave to stand for a few minutes, then drain.
2   Place the onion and lemon juice in a bowl, cover and cook for 3 min. Add 1 × 15ml tbsp (1tbsp) herbs and the fish stock, cover and cook for 3 min.
3   Blend the cornflour with the water, add to the stock and cook for 1 min until thickened. Mix well and stir in the cream. Heat for 15 sec.
4   Spoon the sauce over the herrings, sprinkle with the remaining herbs and serve hot.

Note: *This dish may also be served cold, but allow the sauce to chill, then whisk well before spooning over the cold herring fillets*

DO NOT FREEZE

Red Mullet Niçoise (page 54)

1 spanish onion, sliced
4 herring fillets
2 dill cucumbers, sliced
french dressing, using white
    wine instead of vinegar
    (page 109)

Herring and dill cucumber salad *(serves 4)*   *colour page 19*
POWER LEVEL: 100% (FULL)

Serve as an hors d'oeuvre or as part of a buffet menu

1 Push the onion slices through into rings. Place in a large bowl, cover and cook for 3–4 min, shaking or tossing the onion rings halfway through. The onions should still be slightly crisp.
2 Drain and rinse the onion rings under cold running water. Slice the herring fillets diagonally. Slice the cucumbers.
3 Arrange the herrings in the middle of the serving dish with the cucumber around the edge. Pour over the french dressing to taste and top with the onion rings.
4 Garnish with the chopped parsley before serving cold with brown bread and butter.

DO NOT FREEZE

For garnish: chopped fresh parsley
For serving: brown bread and butter

Kipper

225g (8oz) frozen kipper fillets
1 small onion, chopped
1 lemon, grated rind
1 × 15ml tbsp (1tbsp) lemon
    juice
550ml (1pt) white sauce
    (page 109)
4 eggs, separated
1 × 15ml tbsp (1tbsp) chopped
    parsley
salt and freshly ground black
    pepper
20g (¾oz) gelatine
2 × 15ml tbsp (2tbsp) water

Chilled kipper soufflé *(serves 6)*   *colour page 118*
POWER LEVEL: 100% (FULL)

Serve as a starter or part of a buffet menu

1 Prepare a 14cm (5½in) soufflé dish by tying a double band of greaseproof paper around the outside of the dish to rise 5cm (2in) above the rim of the dish. Secure firmly with string.
2 Place the kipper fillets in a shallow casserole dish. Add the onion, lemon rind and juice. Cover and cook for 5–6 min until tender, turning once halfway through.
3 Skin the fish and blend in a liquidiser or food processor with the onion, lemon rind, juices, white sauce and egg yolks. Stir in the parsley and season to taste.
4 Sprinkle the gelatine onto the water in a small bowl and heat for 10–15 sec. Stir until dissolved, then stir into the fish mixture. Chill until half set.
5 Whisk the egg whites until stiff, then fold into the fish mixture. Pour into the prepared soufflé dish and chill until set.
6 Carefully remove the greaseproof paper and press the chopped parsley around the edges. Garnish the top with lemon butterflies and serve with brown bread and butter.

For garnish: chopped parsley and lemon butterflies
For serving: brown bread and butter

Quick kipper pâté *(serves 4)*
POWER LEVEL: 100% (FULL)

1 Slit the kipper bag. Heat the kippers for 2 min, stand for 5 min.
2 Cook the kippers for 3 min. Skin the fillets and flake the fish. Place in a liquidiser goblet or food processor. Blend until well mixed.
3 Cook the onion in a small covered dish for 1½–2 min, then add to the kipper mixture. Add the other ingredients and seasoning to taste.
4 Pack the mixture into a serving dish and garnish with parsley. Cover and chill in the refrigerator for at least 1 hr before serving. Serve with hot buttered toast.

DO NOT FREEZE

For garnish: sprigs of parsley
For serving: buttered toast

175g (6oz) pkt frozen kipper fillets
1 small onion, chopped
100ml (4fl oz) natural yoghurt
salt and pepper
squeeze of lemon juice
1 × 15ml tbsp (1tbsp) chopped parsley

Lobster

Live lobsters should be killed by conventional methods. This can be done by plunging the fish into large pans of boiling water or court bouillon (a stock for cooking fish) and afterwards cooked for the correct length of time, allowing 10–15 min per 450g (lb) at simmering point. A good fishmonger will often do this for you, but it is only really suitable if the lobster is required to be served cold or boiled. The alternative way is to pierce with the pointed end of a heavy sharp knife right through the natural marked cross on the head, underneath which is the brain. The lobster will be killed instantly. This latter method is best prior to cooking when the lobster is to be served hot, and is preferred by many people. However, the recipes included here are for using cooked lobster, as the microwave cooker will heat the flesh extremely quickly, ensuring practically no loss of flavour.

Lobster newburg *(serves 3–4)*
POWER LEVEL: 100% (FULL) AND 70%

1 Cut the lobster(s) in half. Discard the stomach, intestine and spongy gills. Crack the claws and remove the meat as whole as possible. Detach all the meat from the lobster halves and cut the tail into slices.
2 Melt the butter in a shallow dish for 1 min, add the lobster meat and season well. Cover and cook for 2–3 min, stirring halfway through.
3 Remove lobster and add the madeira or sherry to the dish. Cook, uncovered, for 3–4 min until liquid quantity is reduced by half.
4 Blend the egg yolks with the cream and add to the dish with the lobster. Reduce to 70% setting, cover and cook for 2–3 min until the sauce has thickened. Stir frequently and do not allow to boil.
5 Serve on a bed of boiled rice and garnish with chopped parsley.

DO NOT FREEZE

For serving: boiled rice (page 114)
For garnish: chopped fresh parsley

2 small or 1 large cooked lobster
25g (1oz) butter
salt and white pepper
pinch each cayenne pepper and paprika
4 × 15ml tbsp (4tbsp) madeira wine or sherry
2 egg yolks
150ml (¼pt) single cream

2 small or 1 large cooked lobster
2 × 15ml tbsp (2tbsp) oil
2 small onions, chopped
2 red peppers, deseeded and
    thinly sliced
6 tomatoes, skinned and
    chopped
salt and freshly ground black
    pepper
½ glass white wine
2 × 15ml tbsp (2tbsp) chopped
    parsley
½ × 5ml tsp (½tsp) paprika
1 × 15ml tbsp (1tbsp) brandy
    (optional)

Spanish lobster *(serves 3–4)*
POWER LEVEL: 100% (FULL)

1 Prepare the lobster(s) as described in the recipe for Buttered Lobster (see page 50). Carefully remove the lobster meat from the shell and claws and cut into slices.
2 Place the oil in a shallow dish, stir in the onions, cover and cook for 2 min. Add the peppers, cover and cook for 6 min.
3 Stir in the tomatoes, seasoning and wine, cover and cook for 4–5 min until the sauce is a pulp.
4 Add the lobster meat and carefully turn over in the sauce. Stir in the parsley, paprika and brandy. Cover and heat through for 2 min.
5 Serve hot with boiled rice.

For serving: boiled rice (page 114)

2 small or 1 large cooked lobster
50g (2oz) butter
1 × 15ml tbsp (1tbsp) chopped
    onion
2 × 15ml tbsp (2tbsp) chopped
    parsley
1–2 × 15ml tbsp (1–2tbsp)
    chopped tarragon
4 × 15ml tbsp (4tbsp) white
    wine
275ml (½pt) béchamel sauce
    (page 112)
pinch each dry mustard, salt,
    paprika
3 × 15ml tbsp (3tbsp) grated
    parmesan cheese
2 × 15ml tbsp (2tbsp) browned
    breadcrumbs
slivers of butter

Lobster thermidor *(serves 2 or 4)*   *colour opposite*
POWER LEVEL: 100% (FULL)

1 Remove the lobster meat from the shells, discarding the stomach, intestine and spongy-looking gills. Chop the claw and head meat and cut the meat from the tail into thick slices. Wash the shells.
2 Melt 25g (1oz) butter in a large bowl for 1 min. Add the onion, parsley and tarragon, cover and cook for 1 min. Add the wine and cook, uncovered, for 2–3 min until the onion is tender and the liquid quantity reduced slightly.
3 Stir in the béchamel sauce and mix well with the onion and herbs. Add the lobster meat, seasonings, remaining butter and 2 × 15ml tbsp (2tbsp) of the cheese; cover and heat for 2–3 min.
4 Divide the mixture between the shells. Sprinkle with the remaining cheese and breadcrumbs and top with slivers of butter. Cook, uncovered, for 1½–2 min until heated through; alternatively, brown the top under a hot grill.
5 Serve immediately with lemon wedges and watercress.

DO NOT FREEZE IN THE SHELLS

For garnish: lemon wedges and watercress

Lobster Thermidor (above)

2 small cooked lobsters, 350g
    (12oz) each, approximately
50g (2oz) butter
salt and paprika for sprinkling
1–2 × 15ml tbsp (1–2tbsp)
    lemon juice or cream

Buttered lobster *(serves 2 or 4)*
POWER LEVEL: 100% (FULL)

A delicious way of eating lobster—served hot without rich sauces to mask the delicate flavour

1 Twist off the large claws from the lobster and crack carefully so that the flesh is not crushed.
2 Split the lobsters through from head to tail along the back using a heavy, sharp, pointed knife or cleaver. Remove the intestine (a small tube running through the tail), the stomach (the small sac near the head), and the spongy gills.
3 Melt 15g (½oz) butter for 30 sec. Arrange the half lobsters and claws in a large dish, cut side upwards, and brush the surface with the melted butter.
4 Cover and cook for about 3½–4 min until hot. Allow to stand for 2 min. Sprinkle with a little salt and paprika.
5 Melt the remaining butter for 1½ min, add the lemon juice or cream. This can either be handed separately or poured over the lobster halves before serving.
6 Garnish the lobster halves with parsley and arrange the cracked claws in the centre. Hand brown bread and butter separately.

DO NOT FREEZE

For garnish: parsley sprigs
For serving: brown bread and butter

Mackerel

Mackerel with mushroom stuffing *(serves 2–4)*
POWER LEVEL: 100% (FULL)

1 Clean and bone the mackerel and remove heads. Wash in cold water and dry.
2 Mix together the oil, onion and garlic, cover and cook for 3 min, tossing well halfway through. Stir in the mushrooms, cover and cook for 3 min.
3 Add the breadcrumbs, seasoning and parsley and mix well together. Stuff the mackerel with this mixture.
4 Arrange the mackerel head-to-tail in a large dish, cover and cook for 7–8 min, turning once halfway through if necessary.
5 Serve hot with creamy mustard sauce.

For serving: creamy mustard sauce (page 108/optional)

4 small or 2 large mackerel
1 × 15ml tbsp (1tbsp) oil
1 small onion, finely chopped
1 clove garlic, crushed
100g (4oz) mushrooms, finely chopped
4 × 15ml tbsp (4tbsp) fresh white breadcrumbs
salt and freshly ground black pepper
1 × 15ml tbsp (1tbsp) chopped fresh parsley

Mackerel with fennel sauce *(serves 4)*
POWER LEVEL: 100% (FULL)

1 Clean the fish, remove the heads (and tails if preferred), wash well in cold water and dry.
2 Melt the butter in a large shallow dish for 1–1½ min, place the mackerel head-to-tail in the dish and brush with the melted butter. Season with salt and freshly ground black pepper.
3 Cover and cook for 8–10 min, turning once halfway through, and rearranging the mackerel in the dish by placing the centre ones to the outside. Allow to stand, covered, for 5 min.
4 Garnish with lemon wedges and small bunches of watercress. Serve with fennel sauce handed separately.

For garnish: lemon wedges and watercress
For serving: fennel sauce (page 110)

4 mackerel, 350g (12oz) each, approximately
40g (1½oz) butter
salt and freshly ground black pepper

4 mackerel
15g (½oz) butter, melted
salt and pepper
fine oatmeal or rolled oats
75–100g (3–4oz) butter or
 margarine, melted

Mackerel in oatmeal (serves 4)   colour opposite
POWER LEVEL: 100% (FULL)

The mackerel are cooked in a browning dish

1 Clean the fish and remove the head and tail. Wash in cold water and dry.
2 Brush the fish with 15g (½oz) melted butter, then dip the fish in the oatmeal or rolled oats, pressing the oats well onto the fish.
3 Pre-heat the browning dish for 6–8 min, depending on its size, and add half the melted butter or margarine. Heat for a further 1 min, then add 2 of the fish. Cook, uncovered, for 2 min, turn the fish over, cover and cook for a further 2–3 min. Remove from the dish and keep warm.
4 Remove any drippings from the browning dish, pre-heat for 3–4 min, and cook the remaining 2 fish as described above.
5 Serve hot, sprinkled with plenty of chopped parsley and garnished with lemon wedges.

For garnish: chopped parsley and lemon wedges

25g (1oz) butter
1 small onion, finely chopped
100g (4oz) white breadcrumbs
salt and freshly ground black
 pepper
1 × 15ml tbsp (1tbsp) chopped
 parsley
½ × 5ml tsp (½tsp) dried
 mixed herbs
2–3 × 15ml tbsp (2–3tbsp) hot
 water
4 mackerel, 275–350g
 (10–12oz) each, cleaned
 and boned

Stuffed mackerel with gooseberry sauce (serves 4)
POWER LEVEL: 100% (FULL)

1 Melt the butter in a bowl for 1 min. Add the onion, toss well in the butter, cover and cook for 3–4 min until tender.
2 Stir in the breadcrumbs, seasonings and herbs. Add sufficient hot water to bind the stuffing together.
3 Divide the stuffing between the mackerel and place head-to-tail in a large shallow casserole dish, overlapping slightly to protect the tail ends; alternatively, cover these thinner parts with small smooth pieces of aluminium foil. Cover with greaseproof paper.
4 Cook for 10–12 min, rearranging the mackerel halfway through if necessary by placing the centre ones to the outside. Leave to stand, covered, for 5 min.
5 Place the gooseberry sauce in a serving bowl or jug and heat through if necessary for 2–3 min, although it may also be served cold.
6 Garnish the mackerel with lemon slices and serve with the gooseberry sauce handed separately.

For serving: 275ml (½pt) gooseberry sauce (see page 110)
For garnish: lemon slices

Mackerel in Oatmeal (above)

2 large mackerel, filleted
salt
few drops lemon juice
½ cucumber, peeled and diced
75g (3oz) frozen chopped
   spinach, thawed
few sprigs herbs, ie tarragon
   and chervil
150ml (¼pt) white sauce
   (page 109)
1 egg yolk
1–2 × 15ml tbsp (1–2tbsp)
   cream
salt and pepper

Mackerel in creamy cucumber sauce *(serves 4)*
POWER LEVEL: 100% (FULL)

1 Place the mackerel fillets in a shallow dish, sprinkle with salt and lemon juice. Cover and cook for 4–5 min, then leave to stand for 5 min.
2 Cook the cucumber in a bowl for 3 min, tossing or stirring once halfway through.
3 Add the spinach and herbs to the white sauce, stir well, cover and cook for 2–2½ min. Blend in a liquidiser or rub through a sieve.
4 Drain the fish, adding the liquid to the sauce. Blend the egg yolk with 1 × 15ml tbsp (1tbsp) cream and stir into the sauce with the cucumber. Cook for 1–2 min until slightly thickened, stirring every 30 sec. Do not allow to boil. Adjust seasoning and stir in the remaining cream if required.
5 Spoon the sauce over the mackerel fillets and serve with boiled potatoes.

For serving: boiled potatoes

Red Mullet

4 red mullet
juice ½ lemon
2–3 × 15ml tbsp (2–3tbsp) oil,
   approximately
2 shallots, finely chopped
1 clove garlic, crushed
salt and freshly ground black
   pepper
350g (12oz) tomatoes, fresh
   skinned and chopped, *or*
   450g (1lb) canned tomatoes
2 × 15ml tbsp (2tbsp) chopped
   parsley
1 wine glass white wine

Red mullet provençale *(serves 4)*
POWER LEVEL: 100% (FULL)

1 Clean and scale the fish, remove gills if required. Wash well in cold water, and dry with kitchen paper. Sprinkle with the lemon juice.
2 Heat 2 × 15ml tbsp (2tbsp) oil for 2–3 min until hot. Add the fish, cover and cook for 3 min; turn over in the oil and continue to cook for 2–3 min. Drain and place in a serving dish; keep warm.
3 Add the remaining oil to the dish with the shallots and garlic, cover and cook for 3–4 min. Add seasoning, tomatoes, parsley and wine, cover and cook for 2–3 min.
4 Pour over the fish, cook for a further 1–2 min to boost serving temperature if necessary.
5 Serve with croûtes of toasted french bread.

For serving: croûtes of toasted french bread

4 red mullet
a few sprigs of parsley or thyme
salt and freshly ground black
   pepper
2 × 15ml tbsp (2tbsp) oil
1 clove garlic, crushed
1 × 5ml tsp (1tsp) paprika
1 × 5ml tsp (1tsp) tomato purée
1 wine glass white wine
100g (4oz) black olives

Red mullet niçoise *(serves 4)*   *colour page 45*
POWER LEVEL: 100% (FULL)

This red mullet dish is also good served cold

1 Clean and scale the fish, wash well in cold water, dry and place head-to-tail in a dish with the herbs. Season with salt and freshly ground black pepper.
2 Mix together the oil, garlic, paprika, tomato purée and white wine in a heatproof bowl, cover and cook for 2–3 min, stirring once halfway through.
3 Spoon the sauce over the fish, cover and cook for 5 min, basting the fish with the sauce halfway through. Add the olives to the dish, baste the fish again with the sauce, cover and cook for 1–2 min until heated through.
4 Serve garnished with lemon wedges.

For garnish: lemon wedges

Red mullet in butter *(serves 4)*
POWER LEVEL: 100% (FULL)

4 red mullet
75g (3oz) butter
juice ½ lemon
salt and freshly ground black
    pepper

A popular way of conventionally cooking red mullet is 'en papillote'—in grease-proof paper parcels. In the microwave, it is not necessary to do this as the fish cook in the natural juices anyway, but make sure that they just fit into the dish without too much room to spare

1 Clean and scale the fish, leaving the heads and tails on. Wash thoroughly and dry with kitchen paper.
2 Melt the butter in a shallow dish for 2 min. Lay the fish head-to-tail in the dish and spoon over the melted butter.
3 Sprinkle with lemon juice, a little salt and freshly ground black pepper.
4 Cover and cook for 5–6 min, basting the fish halfway through with the butter and juices. Allow to stand for 2–3 min before serving.
5 Garnish with watercress and serve with boiled potatoes and mixed salad.

For garnish: watercress
For serving: boiled potatoes and mixed salad

Mussels

Moules à la marinière *(serves 2)*   colour page 95
POWER LEVEL: 100% (FULL)

550ml (1pt) mussels
25g (1oz) butter
1 small onion, finely chopped
1 small carrot, diced
1 celery stick, finely chopped
bouquet garni
salt and pepper
1 wine glass white wine
1–2 × 5ml tsp (1–2tsp) flour

Serve as a starter

1 Scrub the mussels and rinse well in cold water. Discard any which are broken or not tightly closed, and scrape away the beards or tufts of hair with a sharp knife.
2 Melt the butter in a large bowl for 1 min. Add the vegetables, cover and cook for 2 min. Add the bouquet garni, seasoning and white wine, cover and cook for 2 min until boiling. Add the mussels, cover and cook for approximately 3–3½ min until the shells are open, tossing well halfway.
3 Place the mussels on a serving dish. Strain the liquid from the mussels into a small bowl and blend in the flour. Cook for 1–2 min until thickened and pour over the mussels.
4 Serve hot, garnished with chopped parsley.

DO NOT FREEZE

For garnish: 2 × 5ml tsp (2tsp) chopped fresh parsley

Seafood pizza *(serves 3–4)*
POWER LEVEL: 100% (FULL)

450g (1lb) pizza dough
    (page 116)
550ml (1pt) tomato sauce
    (page 112)
2 × 300g (10oz) cans or jars
    mussels, drained
50g (2oz) can anchovy fillets
75–100g (3–4oz) black olives
fresh chopped or dried oregano
chopped fresh parsley
2 × 15ml tbsp (2tbsp) olive oil

1 Make the pizza dough. When the dough has been shaped and proved for the second time, add the topping as follows.
2 Spread each round of dough liberally with the tomato sauce. Cover with the mussels, and the drained anchovy fillets which should be split in two lengthways. Top with the black olives.
3 Sprinkle with the herbs and the olive oil (about 1–2 × 5ml tsp/1–2tsp) for each pizza.
4 Cook the smaller pizzas for 5–6 min each, the larger ones for 7–8 min each, giving a quarter turn every 1½ min.

Note: *Peeled prawns may be used instead of the mussels if preferred*

100g (4oz) green streaky bacon
1 onion, chopped
1 stick celery, chopped
1 small green pepper, chopped
2 small potatoes, peeled and
  diced
425ml (¾pt) boiling water
salt and freshly ground black
  pepper
1 bay leaf
40g (1½oz) plain flour
550ml (1pt) milk
300g (10oz) can or jar mussels,
  drained

2.2 litres (4pt) mussels
25g (1oz) butter
1 onion, sliced
1–2 cloves garlic, crushed
1 carrot, finely sliced
bouquet garni
6 peppercorns
1 wine glass white wine
1 wine glass water
450g (1lb) tomatoes, skinned
salt and freshly ground black
  pepper

Mussel chowder (serves 4–6)
POWER LEVEL: 100% (FULL)

This is a substantial dish, delicious on its own or when served with crusty french bread

1 Remove the rind from the bacon and cut the rashers into strips. Place in a large bowl and cook for 2 min.
2 Add the onion, celery and pepper, cover and cook for 3 min.
3 Add the potato, boiling water, seasoning and bay leaf. Cover and cook for 6 min; remove the bay leaf.
4 Blend the flour with a little of the milk and add with the rest to the bacon and vegetables. Mix well together.
5 Cover and cook for approximately 10 min until boiling, whisking every 3 min. Add the mussels to the dish and cook for 3 min.
6 Serve garnished with chopped parsley.

For garnish: 1 × 15ml tbsp (1tbsp) chopped parsley

Mussels with rice (serves 4)
POWER LEVEL: 100% (FULL)

1 Scrub the mussels and rinse well in cold water. Discard any which are broken or not tightly closed, and scrape away the beards or tufts of hair with a sharp knife.
2 Melt the butter in a very large bowl for 1 min. Add the onion, garlic and carrot, cover and cook for 3 min. Add the bouquet garni, peppercorns, wine and water, cover and cook for 3–4 min until boiling.
3 Add the mussels, cover and cook for approximately 6 min until the shells are open, tossing well halfway through. Allow to stand for a few minutes.
4 Cut the tomatoes into quarters and remove the seeds and small hard core.
5 Remove mussels from their shells with a sharp knife and add them to the tomatoes. Strain the liquid from the dish into a jug or small bowl and use some of it with the chicken stock to make the rice pilaf (page 114).
6 When the rice is cooked, fork in the mussels and tomatoes. Adjust seasoning and dot with slivers of butter. If the rice is a little dry, add about 1 × 15ml tbsp (1tbsp) of the mussel liquid.
7 Cover and cook for 1 min to heat through; allow to stand for 5 min before serving.

DO NOT FREEZE

For serving: rice pilaf (page 114 and method 5) and slivers butter

Oysters in Cream (page 58);
Mediterranean Prawn Starter
(page 62)

Oysters

12 lean bacon rashers,
   450–575g (1–1¼lb),
   approximately
12 oysters

Angels on horseback (*serves 6–12*)   *colour page 118*
POWER LEVEL: 100% (FULL)

Serve as a starter or savoury or part of a buffet menu

1   Remove rinds from the bacon rashers and wrap each one around an oyster. Secure with cocktail sticks.
2   Place in a circle on a plate and cook, uncovered, for 8–9 min, turning the plate halfway through if necessary. Drain on kitchen paper.
3   Serve hot on buttered rounds of toast and garnish with watercress.

DO NOT FREEZE

For serving: 12 small slices hot buttered toast
For garnish: watercress

12 oysters in their half shells
6 × 15ml tbsp (6tbsp) double
   cream, approximately
slivers butter
parmesan cheese for sprinkling
paprika for sprinkling

Oysters in cream (*serves 2–3*)   *colour page 57*
POWER LEVEL: 100% (FULL)

1   Loosen the oysters from the shells and arrange the shells containing the oysters in a circle on a large plate or dish.
2   Pour approximately ½ × 15ml tbsp (½tbsp) cream into each one. Top each oyster with a sliver of butter.
3   Sprinkle with parmesan cheese and paprika. Cover and cook for 2–3 min. Allow to stand for 2 min.
4   Serve immediately.

DO NOT FREEZE

15g (½oz) butter
1 clove garlic, crushed with salt
2 rashers back bacon
4 × 15ml tbsp (4tbsp) browned
   breadcrumbs
salt and pepper
12 oysters or 1 can oysters,
   drained

Oysters gratinées (*serves 2*)
POWER LEVEL: 100% (FULL)

Serve as a starter

1   Melt the butter in a bowl for 15 sec, add the garlic, cover and cook for 1 min.
2   Remove the rind from the bacon and cut the rashers into thin strips. Put onto a plate and cook, uncovered, for 3–4 min until the pieces of bacon are crispy. Drain on kitchen paper.
3   Add the browned breadcrumbs to the butter and garlic, toss well in the butter and season lightly.
4   Place the oysters into a serving dish and spoon over the breadcrumbs. Scatter the bacon strips over the top and cook, uncovered, for 1½–2 min if using the canned oysters, or 2½–3 min if using fresh ones. Allow to stand for 3–4 min before serving.
5   Serve garnished with parsley sprigs.

DO NOT FREEZE

For garnish: parsley sprigs

Plaice

Plaice stuffed with prawns (*serves 2*)
POWER LEVEL: 70%

This dish may also be cooked using sole

1   Carefully remove the dark skin from the fish. Do not remove the white skin, head or tail as these serve to keep the fish in shape.
2   With a sharp knife, cut along the centre of the 2 top fillets and raise them away from the bone without detaching them. Using scissors, cut away the backbone and remove.
3   Melt half of the butter in a large shallow dish for 30 sec. Lay the plaice in the dish and brush with butter.
4   Melt the remaining butter in a bowl or dish for 30 sec, add the mushrooms and cook for 2 min. Mix in the béchamel sauce, prawns and cream.
5   Fill the plaice with the prawn mixture and reshape. Protect the thinner parts of the fish with small smooth pieces of aluminium foil.
6   Cover and cook for 6–7 min. Remove foil pieces and, if necessary, cook for a further minute.
7   Drain and serve hot, garnished with bunches of watercress and lemon wedges.

For garnish: watercress and lemon wedges

2 medium whole plaice
25g (1oz) butter
50g (2oz) button mushrooms, quartered
2 × 15ml tbsp (2tbsp) béchamel sauce (page 112)
50g (2oz) peeled prawns
2 × 15ml tbsp (2tbsp) cream

Plaice and mushrooms au gratin (*serves 4*)
POWER LEVEL: 100% (FULL)

1   Lay the plaice fillets head-to-tail in a large buttered shallow dish. Sprinkle with a few drops of lemon juice. Cover and cook for 3–4 min, turning the dish halfway through if necessary.
2   Melt the butter in a bowl or dish for 1 min. Add the mushrooms, season lightly, cover and cook for 3–4 min. Drain the mushrooms and scatter over the fish.
3   Heat the béchamel sauce if necessary, then stir in the cream. Spoon the sauce over the mushrooms and fish.
4   Mix the breadcrumbs with the cheese and sprinkle over the top of the sauce. Heat in the microwave for 2–3 min until the cheese is melted; alternatively, brown under a hot grill.
5   Allow to stand for 2 min before serving.

2 large plaice, filleted
few drops lemon juice
25g (1oz) butter
350g (12oz) button mushrooms, washed and sliced
salt and pepper
275ml (½pt) béchamel sauce (page 112)
150ml (¼pt) single cream
3 × 15ml tbsp (3tbsp) browned breadcrumbs
3 × 15ml tbsp (3tbsp) grated cheddar and parmesan cheese, mixed

Plaice in mushroom sauce (*serves 4*)
POWER LEVEL: 100% (FULL)

1   Wash and dry the fillets, sprinkle with lemon juice and seasoning. Roll up each fillet and place in a casserole dish.
2   Mix the soup and milk or wine together and pour over the fish. Cover and cook for 6–7 min, turning the dish once throughout. Allow to stand for a few minutes.
3   Serve hot with creamed potatoes.

For serving: creamed potatoes (page 113)

4 large plaice fillets, 900g (2lb), approximately
juice ½ lemon
salt and pepper
1 can condensed cream of mushroom soup
1 × 15ml tbsp (1tbsp) milk or white wine

4 plaice, skinned and filleted
salt and pepper
few drops lemon juice
275ml (½pt) white wine sauce
(page 109)

Plaice in wine sauce *(serves 4)*
POWER LEVEL: 100% (FULL)

1 Wash and dry the plaice fillets, sprinkle with salt and pepper and a few drops of lemon juice. Roll up each one and place in a casserole dish. Cover and cook for 3–3½ min, turning the dish halfway through. Allow to stand for 2 min.
2 Heat the sauce if necessary for 2 min. Drain the fish and return to the dish. Spoon the sauce over the plaice.
3 Cut the grapes in half and remove the pips. Garnish the fish with the grapes, lemon twists and toasted croûtes.

DO NOT FREEZE WITH THE GARNISH

For garnish: 8 white grapes, lemon twists and toasted croûtes

8 fillets of plaice, skinned
few drops lemon juice
salt and freshly ground black
    pepper
675g (1½lb) frozen leaf
    spinach, thawed
25g (1oz) butter
275ml (½pt) white sauce
    (page 109)
2 × 15ml tbsp (2tbsp) parmesan
    cheese
paprika for sprinkling

Plaice florentine *(serves 4–8)*   *colour opposite*
POWER LEVEL: 100% (FULL)

1 Fold the fish fillets in half so that the thin end is tucked underneath. Place in a shallow dish and sprinkle with a few drops lemon juice and seasoning. Cover and cook for 3–4 min. Allow to stand for a few minutes.
2 Heat the spinach through for 4 min and beat in the butter; season to taste. Arrange the spinach in a serving dish and the plaice fillets on top.
3 Heat the white sauce if necessary and carefully spoon over each plaice fillet. Sprinkle with parmesan cheese and paprika.
4 Cook, uncovered, for 1–2 min to heat through; alternatively brown under a hot grill.

DO NOT FREEZE

Plaice Florentine (above);
Turbot with Sweetcorn (page 93)

60

Prawns

Mediterranean prawn starter *(serves 3–4)*   *colour page 57*
POWER LEVEL: 100% (FULL)

3 × 15ml tbsp (3tbsp) butter
1–2 cloves garlic, finely
   chopped
4 × 15ml tbsp (4tbsp) dry white
   wine
350g (12oz) king-size prawns,
   heads removed

1   Place the butter, garlic and wine in a large shallow dish. Cover and cook for 2–3 min.
2   Add the prawns, toss in the sauce, cover and cook for 2 min.
3   Allow to stand for 1 min before serving in individual bowls or plates, and garnish with snipped parsley.

For garnish: few sprigs parsley

Prawns creole *(serves 4)*
POWER LEVEL: 100% (FULL)

25g (1oz) butter
1 small onion, finely chopped
1 green pepper, deseeded and
   finely chopped
2–3 × 15ml tbsp (2–3tbsp) flour
675g (1½lb) canned tomatoes,
   roughly chopped
1 × 5ml tsp (1tsp) each dried
   rosemary, thyme and
   oregano
salt and pepper
2 × 5ml tsp (2tsp) sugar
225g (8oz) peeled prawns

1   Melt the butter in a large casserole dish for 1 min. Add the onion and pepper, toss well in the butter, cover and cook for 4–5 min until tender.
2   Stir in the flour until smooth and gradually add the tomatoes; add the herbs, seasoning and sugar.
3   Cover and cook for 5 min, stirring frequently until the sauce has thickened. Allow to stand for 5 min.
4   Stir in the prawns, cover and cook for 1–2 min until heated through. Serve with boiled rice.

For serving: boiled rice (page 114)

Chinese cucumber starter *(serves 4)*
POWER LEVEL: 100% (FULL)

1 large cucumber, washed
40g (1½oz) butter
100g (4oz) button mushrooms,
   washed
1 × 5ml tsp (1tsp) cornflour
75ml (2½fl oz) chicken stock
75ml (2½fl oz) single cream
few drops soy sauce
100g (4oz) peeled prawns

1   Cut the cucumber into 1.25cm (½in) dice, place in a dish, cover and cook for 3 min. Drain.
2   Melt the butter in a bowl for 1–1½ min, add the mushrooms, cover and cook for 2 min. Add the cucumber and cook for 3 min until the vegetables are tender but crisp.
3   Blend the cornflour with the stock, add the cream and soy sauce. Pour over the vegetables and heat for 1–2 min. Stir in the prawns and continue to heat for 1–2 min.
4   Divide the mixture between 4 individual serving dishes and garnish with the chopped herbs and lemon or cucumber twists.
5   Serve hot.

For garnish: chopped fresh chives or dill, lemon or cucumber twists

Note: *Tiny button mushrooms are best, but if the mushrooms are large, cut into slices before cooking*

DO NOT FREEZE

Avocado ring mould with prawns *(serves 4–6)*
POWER LEVEL: 100% (FULL)

Serve as a starter or as part of a summer buffet party

1 Halve and stone the avocado. Scoop out the flesh with a spoon into a large bowl. Add the lemon rind and juice and mash down with a wooden spoon.
2 Add the cream cheese and seasoning and blend well together. If preferred, purée in a blender or pass through a sieve. Add the soured cream.
3 Sprinkle the gelatine over the water in a bowl and heat in the microwave for 15–30 sec until the gelatine is dissolved. Stir until smooth.
4 Pour in a stream onto the avocado mixture, stirring continuously, until blended together. Add a few drops of green food colouring.
5 Pour into a ring mould and chill for several hours in the refrigerator before turning out onto a serving plate or dish.
6 Mix together the mayonnaise, cream and tomato ketchup and stir in the prawns.
7 Pile the prawn mixture into the centre of the ring mould and serve with mixed salad.

DO NOT FREEZE

For serving: mixed salad

1 large avocado pear, ripe
1 lemon, grated rind and juice
75g (3oz) cream cheese
salt and freshly ground black pepper
150ml (¼pt) soured cream
25g (1oz) gelatine
150ml (¼pt) water
few drops green food colouring (optional)
1 rounded 15ml tbsp (1 rounded tbsp) mayonnaise
1 × 15ml tbsp (1tbsp) double cream
1 × 15ml tbsp (1tbsp) tomato ketchup
100g (4oz) peeled prawns

Prawn curry *(serves 4)*   colour page 115
POWER LEVEL: 100% (FULL) AND 50% (DEFROST)

1 Mix together the first 6 ingredients with a little cold water to make a paste.
2 Melt the butter in a large bowl for 1 min. Add the onion, cover and cook for 3 min.
3 Stir in all the remaining ingredients except the prawns. Cover and cook for 3–4 min until thickened, stirring every minute. Reduce to 50% (defrost) setting and cook for a further 5 min. Allow to stand for 5 min.
4 Stir in the prawns and heat through on 50% (defrost) setting for 4 min. Serve with boiled rice.

For serving: boiled rice (page 114)

generous pinch sweet basil
1 × 5ml tsp (1tsp) cumin powder
1 × 5ml tsp (1tsp) chilli powder
½ × 5ml tsp (½tsp) ground turmeric
1 clove garlic, crushed
1 × 15ml tbsp (1tbsp) cornflour
25g (1oz) butter
1 onion, sliced
pinch salt
2 tomatoes, skinned and chopped
2 × 5ml tsp (2tsp) creamed coconut, softened in a little milk
275ml (½pt) fish stock or water
pinch sugar
juice ½ lemon
450g (1lb) peeled prawns

175g (6oz) shortcrust pastry
  (page 116)
25g (1oz) butter or margarine
1 medium onion, peeled and
  finely sliced
1–2 × 5ml tsp (1–2tsp) curry
  powder
275ml (½pt) béchamel sauce
  (page 112)
150ml (¼pt) soured cream
salt and pepper
225g (8oz) peeled prawns
50g (2oz) long grain rice,
  cooked
paprika for sprinkling

Indian-style flan (*serves 6*)
POWER LEVEL: 100% (FULL)

1 Roll out the pastry, line a 20cm (8in) flan dish and bake blind (page 116).
2 Melt the butter or margarine in a bowl, add the onion, toss well and cook for 2–3 min until soft and transparent. Stir in the curry powder and cook for a further minute.
3 Stir in the béchamel sauce, soured cream and seasoning. Reserving a few prawns for garnish, stir the remainder into the sauce.
4 Pour the mixture into the flan case and smooth the top.
5 Arrange the reserved prawns on the top and the cooked rice around the edge of the flan. Sprinkle with paprika.
6 Serve cold with a crisp salad.

DO NOT FREEZE

For serving: green salad

25g (1oz) butter
1 onion, finely chopped
900g (2lb) tomatoes, fresh or
  canned
100g (4oz) canned pimentos,
  chopped
2 × 5ml tsp (2tsp) tomato purée
850ml (1½pt) boiling chicken
  stock
salt and pepper
175g (6oz) peeled prawns
2 × 5ml tsp (2tsp) arrowroot
  (optional)
150ml (¼pt) double cream

Prawn bisque (*serves 6*)   *colour opposite*
POWER LEVEL: 100% (FULL)

This soup may be served hot or chilled

1 Melt the butter in a large bowl for 1 min. Add the onion, toss well in the butter, cover and cook for 4 min until soft.
2 Skin the fresh tomatoes, cut into quarters and remove the seeds, or drain the canned tomatoes if used.
3 Add the tomatoes, pimentos, tomato purée, boiling chicken stock and seasoning. Cover and bring to the boil in the microwave and then cook for 5 min.
4 Stir in the prawns and purée the soup in a blender or food processor. To thicken the soup, blend the arrowroot with a little cold water and add to the soup in the blender or food processor.
5 Chill the soup if it is to be served cold. Whip the cream and stir into the soup before serving.

100g (4oz) butter
2–3 cloves garlic, crushed or
  finely chopped
450g (1lb) peeled prawns, fresh
  or frozen, thawed
salt and freshly ground black
  pepper
2 × 15ml tbsp (2tbsp) chopped
  parsley

Prawns in garlic butter (*serves 4*)   *colour opposite*
POWER LEVEL: 100% (FULL)

This makes a delicious starter to a meal, but could also be used as a light supper dish

1 Place the butter in a bowl or dish, cover and heat for 2–2½ min until melted. Add the garlic, cover and cook for 1 min.
2 Add the prawns and toss well in the butter and garlic. Season lightly to taste and stir in the parsley.
3 Cover and cook for 3–4 min until heated through. Leave to stand for 1 min.
4 Serve hot in individual au gratin dishes with crusty french bread.

DO NOT FREEZE

For serving: crusty french bread

Prawn Bisque (above);
Prawns in Garlic Butter (above)

1 small cauliflower, cut into
   florets
4 × 15ml tbsp (4tbsp) salted
   water
225g (8oz) peeled prawns
1 green chilli, minced
4 spring onions, minced
275ml (½pt) mayonnaise
   (page 108)
½ × 5ml tsp (½tsp) garam
   masala
lettuce leaves

Curried prawn salad (*serves 4*)
POWER LEVEL: 100% (FULL)

1   Place the cauliflower florets in a bowl with the salted water. Cover and cook for 6–8 min until tender but still crisp. Shake the bowl once or twice throughout. Drain and rinse in cold water.
2   Add the prawns to the cauliflower. Mix the chilli and spring onions with the mayonnaise and garam masala, combine with the cauliflower and prawns.
3   Arrange a bed of lettuce leaves on a serving dish and pile the salad on the top.
4   Chill before serving, garnished with chopped herbs.

DO NOT FREEZE

For garnish: chopped fresh herbs

8 small courgettes, trimmed
   and washed
25g (1oz) butter
1 onion, finely chopped
4 tomatoes, skinned
1 × 5ml tsp (1tsp) paprika
salt and freshly ground black
   pepper
225g (8oz) shelled prawns
275ml (½pt) béchamel sauce
   (page 112)
50g (2oz) grated parmesan
   cheese
paprika for sprinkling

Courgettes maison (*serves 4 or 8*)
POWER LEVEL: 100% (FULL) AND 50% (DEFROST)

1   Place the courgettes in a large dish, cover and cook for 4–5 min. Rinse in cold water.
2   Cutting lengthways, remove a thin slice from the top of each courgette. Discard the slice. Scoop out the flesh from each courgette and chop finely.
3   Melt the butter in a bowl for 1 min. Add the onion, cover and cook for 2 min.
4   Remove the seeds from the tomatoes, chop the flesh and add to the onions with the flesh from the courgettes, paprika and seasonings. Cover and cook for 3 min.
5   Stir the prawns with the mixture and divide between the courgette cases.
6   Cover the dish and cook for a further 3–4 min.
7   Mix the béchamel sauce with half the cheese and spoon over the courgettes. Sprinkle the remaining cheese and paprika over the top of the sauce.
8   Cook, uncovered, for 5 min on 50% (defrost) setting until heated through.

FREEZE THE SAUCE SEPARATELY. FINISH AND GARNISH JUST BEFORE SERVING

Salmon

Salmon-stuffed pancakes (*serves 4–8*)
POWER LEVEL: 100% (FULL)

1 Stir the salmon, mustard and onion into the white sauce. Season to taste.
2 Spread an equal amount of sauce on each pancake and roll up. Lay the pancakes in a shallow serving dish and moisten with the lemon juice.
3 Cover the dish with clingfilm and cook in the microwave for 8 min, giving a quarter turn every 2 min.
4 Top with soured cream and sprinkle with the chopped chives. Serve immediately.

For garnish: 2 × 15ml tbsp (2tbsp) chopped chives

198g (7oz) can salmon, drained and flaked
1 × 5ml tsp (1tsp) mustard
1 × 15ml tbsp (1tbsp) onion, finely chopped
275ml (½pt) white sauce (page 109)
salt and pepper
8 × 20cm (8in) cooked pancakes (page 117)
2 × 15ml tbsp (2tbsp) lemon juice
150ml (¼pt) soured cream

Salmon with prawns in cream (*serves 4*)
POWER LEVEL: 100% (FULL)

1 Wipe the salmon cutlets. Place the butter in a large shallow dish and heat for 1 min until melted.
2 Brush the butter around the dish and add the salmon cutlets with the thicker parts towards the outside of the dish. Fill the cavities with the prawns. Brush the tops of the salmon cutlets and prawns with the butter.
3 Sprinkle with freshly ground black pepper, cover the dish and cook for 7 min. Allow to stand for 2 min.
4 Place the cream in a jug or bowl and heat for 1½ min. Pour the cream over the salmon and prawns, cover the dish and cook for 2 min. Allow to stand for 2 min.
5 Garnish with lemon wedges and sprigs of parsley and serve with buttered cucumber or a cucumber salad.

DO NOT FREEZE

For garnish: lemon wedges and sprigs of parsley
For serving: buttered cucumber (page 113) or cucumber salad

4 × 175g (6oz) salmon cutlets, 2.5cm (1in) thick, approximately
25g (1oz) butter
100g (4oz) peeled prawns, fresh, or frozen, thawed
freshly ground black pepper
275ml (½pt) single cream

100g (4oz) butter
175g (6oz) savoury biscuits or
  crackers, crumbed
50g (2oz) cheese, finely grated

For the filling:

150ml (¼pt) béchamel sauce
  (page 112)
salt and freshly ground black
  pepper
225g (8oz) canned salmon,
  flaked
½ lemon, grated rind and juice
75ml (2½fl oz) mayonnaise
150ml (¼pt) double cream,
  whipped

2 × 200–225g (7–8oz) salmon
  steaks
salt and pepper
150ml (¼pt) white wine sauce
  (page 109)
1 egg yolk
3 × 15ml tbsp (3tbsp) single
  cream

15g (½oz) butter
1 small onion, finely chopped
½ stick celery, finely sliced
200g (7oz) can salmon
75g (3oz) fresh brown
  breadcrumbs
salt and pepper
1–2 × 15ml tbsp (1–2tbsp)
  cream
3 medium avocados, ripe
1 × 15ml tbsp (1tbsp) lemon
  juice
paprika for sprinkling

Smoked Haddock Pâté (page 38);
Salmon-stuffed Avocados (above)

Salmon quiche *(serves 6–8)*
POWER LEVEL: 100% (FULL)

1 Melt the butter in a bowl for 2–3 min. Mix together the biscuit crumbs, butter and grated cheese and press well into the base and sides of a 20cm (8in) flan dish. Chill thoroughly.
2 Mix together the remaining ingredients and pour into the prepared flan case.
3 Smooth the top and chill. Garnish with cucumber slices and chopped parsley before serving.

DO NOT FREEZE

For garnish: cucumber slices and chopped parsley

Salmon with white wine sauce *(serves 2)*
POWER LEVEL: 50% (DEFROST)

1 Wash steaks, place in a dish and sprinkle with salt and pepper. Cover with clingfilm and cook for 10–12 min, turning once.
2 Make up the white wine sauce as directed, using the salmon juices. Cool sauce slightly.
3 While the sauce is cooling, reheat the salmon steaks in a serving dish for 2 min.
4 Stir egg yolk and cream into sauce. Check and adjust seasoning.
5 Pour the sauce over the salmon. Sprinkle with a few prepared shrimps or prawns and garnish with parsley and lemon butterflies.

FREEZE THE SAUCE SEPARATELY

For garnish: shrimps or prawns, parsley and lemon butterflies

Salmon-stuffed avocados *(serves 6)*   *colour opposite*
POWER LEVEL: 100% (FULL)

1 Melt the butter in a large bowl for 30 sec. Stir in the onion and celery, cover and cook for 3–3½ min until transparent.
2 Place the contents of the can of salmon into a bowl and mash well. Add to the onion and celery together with the breadcrumbs. Season to taste and stir in the cream.
3 Cut the avocados in half, remove the stones and scoop most of the flesh from the shells with a spoon, leaving a 6–13mm (¼–½in) thick shell. Mash down the flesh with a wooden spoon and mix in the lemon juice. Add to the salmon mixture and stir well.
4 Divide the filling between the 6 avocado shells and sprinkle with paprika.
5 Arrange in a circle on a plate or on the microwave cooker shelf and cook, uncovered, for 7–8 min, turning the plate or rearranging the avocados halfway through.
6 Serve with croûtes of toasted french bread.

For serving: croûtes of toasted french bread

25g (1oz) butter
4 salmon steaks, 175g (6oz)
    each, approximately
salt and pepper
few drops lemon juice
hollandaise sauce (page 109)

Salmon steaks with hollandaise sauce *(serves 4)*
POWER LEVEL: 100% (FULL)

One of the best ways of serving salmon for a light summer lunch

1 Melt the butter in a shallow casserole dish for 1 min.
2 Wash the salmon steaks and dry. Place in the dish and brush with the melted butter. Sprinkle with salt and pepper and a few drops of lemon juice.
3 Cover and cook for 6–7 min, turning the dish or rearranging the salmon steaks halfway through. Allow to stand for a few minutes, then drain off the juices.
4 Make the hollandaise sauce and place in a warm sauce boat or jug. Arrange the salmon steaks on a serving dish or plate and garnish with lemon twists and parsley sprigs.
5 Serve hot with boiled potatoes which have been tossed in melted butter and chopped parsley, and broccoli or buttered cucumber. Hand the hollandaise sauce separately.

Salmon steaks with fennel sauce *(serves 4)*   colour page 111

Follow the cooking method for the salmon steaks as given above and serve hot with fennel sauce (page 110).

Salmon steaks with mayonnaise *(serves 4)*

Follow the cooking method for the salmon steaks as given above, omitting the melted butter. Leave until cool, then refrigerate until cold. Garnish as above and serve with mayonnaise (page 108).

For garnish: lemon twists and parsley sprigs
For serving: boiled new potatoes and broccoli or buttered cucumber (page 113)

Salmon trout

1 salmon trout, 900g (2lb)
    approximately
salt and pepper
2 bay leaves
25g (1oz) butter
juice ½ lemon

Baked salmon trout *(serves 4–6)*
POWER LEVEL: 100% (FULL)

Serve as a starter or a main course

1 Clean the salmon trout; the head and tail may be removed if preferred, depending also on the size and length of the fish.
2 Wash the fish well and dry. Sprinkle with salt and pepper and place the bay leaves inside the fish. Place the fish on a sheet of greaseproof paper.
3 Melt the butter for 1 min in a bowl and use this to coat thoroughly the salmon trout. Sprinkle with the lemon juice.
4 Wrap the fish tightly in the greaseproof paper and place on the microwave cooker shelf.
5 Cook for 7–8 min, turning the fish over and around once halfway through if necessary. Allow to stand for 4–5 min.
6 Unwrap the fish, remove bay leaves, and serve garnished with cucumber or lemon twists. Serve the hollandaise or fennel sauce separately.

For garnish: cucumber or lemon twists
For serving: hollandaise sauce or fennel sauce (pages 109 and 110/optional)

Salmon trout angers (*serves 4*)
POWER LEVEL: 100% (FULL) AND 70%

1 Clean the salmon trout and remove the head and tail. Wash well in cold water and dry. Place in a large casserole dish.
2 Measure the white wine and make up to 275ml (½pt) with water. Add this to the fish with lemon juice, seasoning and bouquet garni. Cover and cook for 9–10 min, turning the dish or rearranging the fish halfway through if necessary. Leave to stand for a few minutes.
3 Melt the 15g (½oz) butter in a bowl for 30 sec, add the shallot or onion, cover and cook for 2–3 min. Drain off the hot liquid from the fish and add to the onion. Cook, uncovered, for 6–8 min until the liquid is reduced by about half.
4 Blend the egg yolks with the cream and add to the sauce. Reduce to 70% setting and heat without boiling for about 1½–2 min, stirring every 30 sec until the sauce has thickened.
5 Beat the unsalted butter into the hot sauce a little at a time.
6 Remove the skin carefully from the fish and place on to a hot serving dish or platter. Coat the salmon trout with the sauce and serve hot with the buttered cucumber arranged on either side of the fish.

DO NOT FREEZE

For serving: buttered cucumber (page 113)

1 salmon trout, 900g (2lb), approximately
2 wine glasses white wine
water
few drops lemon juice
salt and pepper
bouquet garni
15g (½oz) butter
1 shallot or small onion, finely chopped
3 egg yolks
3 × 15ml tbsp (3tbsp) double cream
25g (1oz) unsalted butter

Salmon trout in aspic (*serves 6*)   *colour page 15*
POWER LEVEL: 100% (FULL)

This dish makes an excellent centrepiece for a formal buffet or may be served as a starter. A large pink trout or small salmon can be cooked and served in the same way

1 Clean the fish, leave whole and wash in cold water. Dry with kitchen paper and cook as for Baked Salmon Trout.
2 Leave to cool slightly and then refrigerate until cold.
3 Remove the skin from the fish, leaving on the head and tail, and place on a cooling tray with a large plate underneath.
4 Make the aspic jelly according to the packet instructions and, when it is beginning to thicken, coat the top of the fish thinly.
5 Decorate the fish, using thin strips of radishes and olives, diamonds or strips of tomato skins and lemon rinds, thin cucumber slices or strips of skin, parsley sprigs and peeled shrimps or prawns.
6 Coat with another layer of aspic jelly, allow to set and add more layers, leaving to set in between, until the decorations are held in place.
7 Carefully transfer the fish to a serving platter and chill.
8 Leave any drippings of aspic jelly on the plate beneath to set, then chop with a sharp knife and use as a garnish around the salmon trout.
9 Serve with a mixed salad and mayonnaise.

DO NOT FREEZE

For decoration: radishes, stuffed olives, tomato skins, pared lemon rind, cucumber, parsley, peeled shrimps or prawns
For serving: mixed salad and mayonnaise (page 108)

1 salmon trout *or* large pink trout *or* small salmon, 900g (2lb), approximately
425ml (¾pt) aspic jelly

Sardines

900g (2lb) fresh sardines
2 lemons
2 tomatoes, sliced
salt and freshly ground black
    pepper
75ml (2½fl oz) oil
1 × 15ml tbsp (1tbsp) chopped
    parsley
1 × 5ml tsp (1tsp) chopped
    oregano

Baked sardines *(serves 4)*   *colour opposite*
POWER LEVEL: 50% (DEFROST)

1   Clean the sardines and remove the heads if required. Wash well and dry. Arrange head-to-tail in a large shallow dish.
2   Slice 1 lemon and squeeze the juice from the other. Place the lemon and tomato slices alternately between the fish. Sprinkle with salt and pepper.
3   Spoon the lemon juice and oil over the fish and scatter with the herbs.
4   Cook, uncovered, for 10–12 min, rearranging the sardines or turning the dish halfway through if necessary.
5   Serve hot or cold.

20cm (8in) flan case (page 116)
3 cans sardines, drained
3 tomatoes, skinned
salt and freshly ground black
    pepper
275ml (½pt) milk
2 eggs

Sardine and tomato flan *(serves 6)*
POWER LEVEL: 100% (FULL) AND 50% (DEFROST)

1   Cook the flan case and arrange the sardines in the base. Slice the tomatoes thinly and place over the top of the sardines. Sprinkle well with salt and freshly ground black pepper.
2   Heat the milk for 2 min. Beat the eggs and whisk in the milk and a little more seasoning to taste. Pour into the flan case.
3   Reduce to 50% (defrost) setting and cook for 12–15 min until the filling is set. It does not matter if it is still a little uncooked as it will finish setting during its standing time. Allow to stand for 10–15 min.
4   Serve hot or warm, garnished with tomato slices.

DO NOT FREEZE

For garnish: tomato slices

2 × 100g (4oz) cans sardines
salt and freshly ground black
    pepper
2 × 15ml tbsp (2tbsp) chopped
    fresh mixed herbs
2 × 15ml tbsp (2tbsp) capers or
    gherkins, chopped
450g (1lb) tomatoes, skinned
4 × 15ml tbsp (4tbsp) browned
    breadcrumbs
50–75g (2–3oz) cheese, grated

Sardines with tomatoes *(serves 4)*
POWER LEVEL: 70% AND 100% (FULL)

Serve hot or cold for lunch or supper

1   Drain the sardines and reserve the oil. Bone the sardines if preferred, and arrange the fish on the base of a suitable microwave au gratin or pie dish.
2   Sprinkle with seasoning, herbs and capers or gherkins, and a little of the reserved oil.
3   Slice the tomatoes thickly, arrange on top of the sardines and sprinkle over a little more salt and pepper and the remaining oil.
4   Cover and cook for 5½–6½ min on 70% setting. Mix the breadcrumbs with the cheese and sprinkle over the top of the tomatoes. Cook, uncovered, on 100% (full) setting for 2 min.
5   Allow to stand for 3–4 min before garnishing with a bay leaf and serving with crusty bread and butter.

For garnish: 1 bay leaf
For serving: crusty bread and butter

Baked Sardines (above)

2 × 120g (4¼oz) cans sardines
4 slices toast
butter, for spreading
2 tomatoes, sliced

Sardines on toast (serves 2–4)
POWER LEVEL: 100% (FULL)

1 Drain the sardines.
2 Butter the slices of toast and arrange the sardines on top.
3 Garnish the toast with slices of tomato and heat for 2 mins. (If cooking 1 slice heat for 30–45 sec, 2 for 1–1½ min.)

DO NOT FREEZE

1 × 15ml tbsp (1tbsp) oil
450g (1lb) fresh sardines, cleaned and washed
2–3 cloves garlic, finely chopped
juice ½ lemon
1 wine glass white wine

Sardines à la granada (serves 4)
POWER LEVEL: 100% (FULL)

1 Heat the oil in a shallow casserole for 2 min. Dry the sardines and place head-to-tail in the oil. Sprinkle with garlic and add lemon juice and wine.
2 Cover and cook for 4–5 min, turning the dish or rearranging the sardines if necessary halfway through. Allow to stand for 5 min.
3 Sprinkle with chopped parsley and serve hot as a starter.

For garnish: 1 × 15ml tbsp (1tbsp) chopped parsley

Scallops

3 × 15ml tbsp (3tbsp) oil
675g (1½lb) frozen scallops, thawed
425g (15oz) can asparagus spears
salt and freshly ground black pepper
2 × 15ml tbsp (2tbsp) dry sherry
½ × 5ml tsp (½tsp) sugar
3 × 5ml tsp (3tsp) cornflour
150ml (¼pt) single cream (optional)

Scallops with asparagus (serves 4–6)
POWER LEVEL: 100% (FULL)

1 Place the oil in a large casserole with the scallops. Cover and cook for 4 min.
2 Drain the can of asparagus and reserve 3 × 15ml tbsp (3tbsp) of the liquid.
3 Cut half of the asparagus spears into 2.5cm (1in) pieces and add to the scallops. Mix together well.
4 Add seasoning, dry sherry and the sugar. Mix well, cover and cook for 3 min.
5 Blend the cornflour with the reserved asparagus liquid and stir into the scallops and asparagus. Cover and cook for about 2 min until thickened. Adjust seasoning and stir in the cream, if used.
6 Heat the reserved asparagus spears for 1 min and use to garnish the dish. Serve hot.

DO NOT FREEZE

Scallop and mushroom pie *(serves 6–8)*
POWER LEVEL: 100% (FULL)

This makes an excellent fish course or main course for a dinner party

1 Lightly grease a large shallow round ovenware dish.
2 Cut each scallop into 4, place with the milk and seasonings in a bowl and cook for 3–4 min. Drain and reserve the milk.
3 Melt 25g (1oz) butter for 1 min, stir in the flour until smooth. Gradually stir in the reserved milk.
4 Cook for 3–4 min until thick, stirring every minute. Beat well until smooth. Mix in the scallops, mushrooms and the wine.
5 Cover with piped creamed potatoes and top with slivers of the remaining butter.
6 Cook for 6–8 min or until heated through, turning every 2 min.
7 Garnish with parsley and serve hot with a side salad.

For garnish: parsley sprigs
For serving: mixed salad

Note: *King-size prawns may replace the scallops. Peel the prawns and add to the sauce, made from the butter, flour and milk, with the mushrooms and wine. Continue as above*

16 scallops, cleaned
275ml (½pt) milk
salt and freshly ground black pepper
50g (2oz) butter
25g (1oz) flour
175g (6oz) mushrooms, washed and sliced
150ml (¼pt) dry white wine
450g (1lb) creamed potatoes (page 113)

8 scallops and their shells (or individual shell dishes)
150ml (¼pt) white wine
1 small onion, grated
salt and freshly ground black pepper
1 bay leaf
225g (8oz) mushrooms, finely sliced
50g (2oz) butter
50g (2oz) flour
200ml (7½fl oz) milk
150ml (¼pt) single cream
1 egg yolk
few drops lemon juice
75g (3oz) cheese, grated
paprika for sprinkling

Coquilles saint-jacques (*serves 4 or 8*)
POWER LEVEL: 100% (FULL)

Use either the deep shells or individual shell dishes for cooking and serving the scallops

1 Wash and dry the scallops and their shells, if used, and put to one side.
2 Place the white wine in a large bowl with the onion, seasoning and bay leaf. Cover and cook for 3 min, stirring once halfway through.
3 Add the mushrooms and scallops, cover and cook for 5 min, stirring once halfway through. Leave to stand.
4 Melt the butter in a large bowl for 1½ min and stir in the flour. When blended, gradually add the milk. Season lightly, cover and cook for 4 min, stirring every minute until the sauce thickens.
5 Blend the cream and egg yolk and add to the sauce with a few drops of lemon juice. Remove the bay leaf from the mushroom and scallop mixture. Add the mixture to the sauce, mixing together well.
6 Divide the mixture between the 8 scallop shells, ensuring that 1 scallop is placed into each.
7 Sprinkle with grated cheese and heat for 2–3 min until the cheese is melted, then sprinkle with paprika. Alternatively, heat through and brown the top under a hot grill.
8 Allow 1 or 2 per person and serve with brown bread and butter.

DO NOT FREEZE

For serving: brown bread and butter

8 scallops
few drops lemon juice
40g (1½oz) butter
1 small onion, chopped
225g (8oz) mushrooms, chopped
1 × 15ml tbsp (1tbsp) chopped fresh parsley
salt and freshly ground black pepper
4 × 15ml tbsp (4tbsp) browned breadcrumbs
slivers butter

Scallops gratinées (*serves 4*)   *colour opposite*
POWER LEVEL: 100% (FULL)

1 If the scallops are in their shells, remove them, wash and keep the shells. Rinse scallops in cold water and place in a shallow dish. Sprinkle on the lemon juice, cover and cook for 2–3 min.
2 Melt half the butter for about 30 sec, add the onion, toss well in the butter. Cover and cook for 3 min. Add the mushrooms and rest of the butter. Cover and cook for 3–4 min until tender, tossing or stirring well halfway through. Drain off excess liquid, stir the parsley into the vegetables and season to taste.
3 Divide half the mixture between 4 of the shells or individual dishes. Place 2 drained scallops into each shell or dish and cover with the remaining mushroom mixture.
4 Sprinkle with breadcrumbs and dot with slivers of butter. Return shells or dishes to the microwave and cook, uncovered, for 1½–2 min to heat through. Alternatively, brown under a hot grill.

DO NOT FREEZE IN THE SHELLS

For garnish: lemon twists and parsley sprigs

Whiting with Orange Sauce (page 94); Scallops Gratinées (above)

Scampi

25g (1oz) butter
450g (1lb) peeled scampi
1 × 5ml tsp (1tsp) paprika
1 glass sherry
3 egg yolks
225ml (8fl oz) double cream
4 tomatoes, skinned and
    quartered
salt and freshly ground black
    pepper

Scampi in cream sauce (*serves 4*)
POWER LEVEL: 100% (FULL) AND 70%

1 Melt the butter in a dish for 1 min, add the scampi, cover and cook for
   2 min. Stir in the paprika, cover and cook for 1 min.
2 Heat the sherry for about 1 min until hot. Remove the cover from the
   scampi, ignite the sherry and pour over the scampi. Do not ignite in the
   microwave.
3 Remove the scampi from the dish, return the dish to the microwave and
   cook, uncovered, for about 4 min to reduce the liquid quantity by half.
4 Blend the egg yolks with the cream and add to the dish with the scampi,
   tomatoes and seasoning. Mix together well.
5 Reduce to 70% setting, cover and cook for 3–4 min until heated through
   and the sauce has thickened sufficiently to coat the back of a spoon. Stir
   frequently and do not allow to boil.
6 Adjust seasoning and serve with boiled rice.

DO NOT FREEZE

For serving: boiled rice (page 114)

15g (½oz) butter
225g (8oz) peeled scampi or
    prawns
few drops of lemon juice
275ml (½pt) béchamel sauce
    (page 112)
1 × 15ml tbsp (1tbsp) browned
    breadcrumbs
1 × 15ml tbsp grated parmesan
    cheese

Scampi au gratin (*serves 2–4*)
POWER LEVEL: 100% (FULL)

1 Melt the butter in a bowl or dish for 30 sec. Add the scampi, toss well in
   the butter, cover and cook for 1½–2 min.
2 Drain the scampi and place in a serving dish or individual au gratin
   dishes, and sprinkle with a few drops of lemon juice.
3 If necessary, heat the sauce through and spoon over the scampi. Sprinkle
   with browned breadcrumbs and parmesan cheese.
4 Cook, uncovered, for 1–2 min until heated through; alternatively brown
   the top under a hot grill.
5 Serve hot, garnished with lemon twists and parsley sprigs.

For garnish: lemon twists and parsley sprigs

25g (1oz) butter
1 onion, chopped
1 clove garlic, chopped
397g (14oz) can tomatoes,
    drained
5 × 15ml tbsp (5tbsp) dry white
    wine
salt and pepper
pinch of sugar
1 × 15ml tbsp (1tbsp) chopped
    parsley
225g (8oz) peeled scampi

Scampi provençale (*serves 4*)
POWER LEVEL: 100% (FULL)

1 Melt the butter in a casserole dish for 1 min. Toss the onion and garlic in
   the butter and cook for 4 min.
2 Add tomatoes, wine, seasoning, sugar and parsley. Stir well and heat for
   3 min.
3 Add the scampi to the sauce, cover and cook for 2–3 min, stirring once
   halfway through. Allow to stand for 2–3 min.
4 Serve hot with boiled rice.

For serving: boiled rice (page 114)

Scampi in wine sauce *(serves 4)*
POWER LEVEL: 100% (FULL)

1 Melt 25g (1oz) butter in a bowl or dish for 1 min. Add the scampi, seasoning, paprika and lemon juice; cover and cook for 3 min, stirring once halfway through.
2 Drain off the scampi and arrange in a serving dish. Keep warm.
3 Add the white wine sauce to the cooking liquor from the scampi and stir in the double cream. Cover and heat through for 2–3 min, stirring once halfway through.
4 Melt the remaining 25g (1oz) butter for 1 min, add the tomatoes, asparagus tips and mushrooms, cover and cook for 2–3 min. Allow to stand for a few minutes.
5 Spoon the sauce over the scampi, cover and heat through for 1 min. Drain the vegetables for the garnish and arrange over the top of the sauce. Serve hot.

DO NOT FREEZE

For garnish: 2 tomatoes, skinned and quartered, seeds removed; 12 asparagus tips, fresh, canned or frozen, thawed; 50g (2oz) button mushrooms

50g (2oz) butter
450g (1lb) peeled scampi
salt and freshly ground black pepper
pinch paprika
few drops lemon juice
275ml (½pt) white wine sauce (page 109)
75ml (2½fl oz) double cream

Scampi italian-style *(serves 4–6)*
POWER LEVEL: 100% (FULL)

1 Place the butter in a large dish or bowl, cover and heat for 1½–2 min. Stir in the courgettes and pepper, cover and cook for 4 min, shaking the dish once halfway through. Remove the vegetables.
2 Add onion and garlic to the dish, cover and cook for 5 min. Add the contents of the can of tomatoes or fresh tomatoes quartered, wine, sugar, parsley and seasoning. Cover and cook for 6–7 min.
3 Add scampi or prawns with the courgettes and pepper, cover and cook for 4–5 min.
4 Arrange the sliced cheese over the top and cook, uncovered, for about 3 min until the cheese is melted. Alternatively, brown under a hot grill.
5 Serve hot with boiled rice.

For serving: boiled rice (page 114)

50g (2oz) butter
2 courgettes, sliced
1 small green pepper, deseeded and cut into strips
1 medium onion, chopped
2 cloves garlic, crushed
225g (8oz) tomatoes, canned, or fresh, skinned
75ml (2½fl oz) dry white wine
1 × 5ml tsp (1tsp) sugar
1 × 15ml tbsp (1tbsp) chopped parsley
salt and freshly ground black pepper
450g (1lb) peeled scampi or prawns, fresh or frozen, thawed
100g (4oz) mozzarella cheese, thinly sliced

Shrimps

2 avocado pears, ripe
few drops of lemon juice
100g (4oz) cream cheese
100g (4oz) canned shrimps,
    drained
freshly ground black pepper
1–2 × 15ml tbsp (1–2tbsp)
    browned breadcrumbs

Shrimp-stuffed avocados *(serves 4)*
POWER LEVEL: 100% (FULL)

1 Cut the avocados in half, remove the stones and brush the flesh of each half with a little lemon juice.
2 Place the avocado halves in a microwave dish with the narrow ends towards the centre. Cover with a lid or clingfilm, slit with the pointed end of a sharp knife.
3 Place in the microwave and cook for 5–7 min until soft, depending on the ripeness of the avocados. Allow to stand for a few minutes.
4 Meanwhile, cream the cheese until smooth. Stir the shrimps into the cheese and add freshly ground black pepper to taste.
5 Uncover the avocados and divide the shrimp and cheese mixture between the 4 halves. Sprinkle with the browned breadcrumbs and heat for 1–2 min—just long enough to heat the topping.
6 Serve hot with lemon wedges.

DO NOT FREEZE

For serving: lemon wedges

225g (8oz) frozen shrimps or
    prawns, thawed
225g (8oz) unsalted or clarified
    butter
½ × 5ml tsp (½tsp) dried basil
pepper to taste

Potted shrimps *(serves 4)*
POWER LEVEL: 100% (FULL)

1 Put the shrimps in a bowl, cover and heat in the microwave for 30 sec. Stand for 1 min, then heat for 1 min.
2 Place about 150g (5oz) of butter in a bowl and melt for 3 min. Liquidise or blend the shrimps, melted butter and seasonings to give a smooth paste.
3 Press mixture firmly into a small dish and chill for ½ hr.
4 Melt the remaining butter for 2 min. Smooth the top of the shrimp mixture and pour over the butter. Cover and chill in the refrigerator.
5 Serve garnished with parsley sprigs and lemon slices.

DO NOT FREEZE

For garnish: parsley sprigs and lemon slices

350g (12oz) tagliatelle or egg
    noodles
25g (1oz) butter
1 clove garlic, crushed
1 stick celery, finely chopped
1 small green pepper, deseeded
    and finely chopped
25g (1oz) flour
salt and pepper
275ml (½pt) milk, or milk and
    white wine mixed
350g (12oz) peeled shrimps or
    prawns, fresh or canned

*Smoked Fish and Prawn Lasagne
(page 96); Tagliatelle with Shrimp
Sauce (above)*

Tagliatelle with shrimp sauce *(serves 4)*   *colour opposite*
POWER LEVEL: 100% (FULL)

1 Cook the tagliatelle or noodles as described on page 114.
2 Melt the butter in a large bowl for 1 min, stir in the garlic, celery and green pepper, cover and cook for 4–5 min until tender.
3 Stir in the flour and seasoning. Gradually add the milk or milk and wine. Cook for 3–4 min until thickened, stirring every minute.
4 Stir in the shrimps or prawns, and cook for 1–2 min until heated through.
5 Drain the tagliatelle and arrange in a serving dish or platter. Pour over the sauce and garnish with a few shrimps or prawns. Serve hot, handing the cheese separately.

FREEZE THE SAUCE SEPARATELY

For garnish: few shrimps or prawns
For serving: grated parmesan cheese

12 large firm tomatoes
40g (1½oz) butter or margarine
1 onion, peeled and finely
   chopped
175g (6oz) peeled shrimps
100g (4oz) cooked rice
   (page 114)
1 × 15ml tbsp (1tbsp) single
   cream or top of the milk
2 × 5ml tsp (2tsp)
   worcestershire sauce
2 × 15ml tbsp (2bsp) chopped
   parsley
salt and freshly ground black
   pepper
50g (2oz) cheese, grated
1 × 15ml tbsp (1tbsp) fresh
   breadcrumbs

Shrimp-stuffed tomatoes *(serves 6)*
POWER LEVEL: 100% (FULL)

Serve as a starter or as a main course with vegetables or rice

1 Cut a thin slice from the top of each tomato and scoop out the flesh.
2 Melt the butter or margarine in a bowl for 1½ min, toss in the onion and cook for 3–4 min.
3 Stir in the shrimps, rice, cream or top of the milk, worcestershire sauce and parsley. Season to taste.
4 Fill the tomato cases with the mixture and place in a shallow round serving dish.
5 Cover and cook for 4–5 min until heated through.
6 Mix together the cheese and breadcrumbs and sprinkle over the top of the tomatoes. Cook, uncovered, for 1½–2 min until the cheese is melted.
7 Serve hot, garnished with parsley sprigs.

For garnish: sprigs of parsley

Skate

675–900g (1½–2lb) skate
275ml (½pt) milk
béchamel sauce (see method 2)
50g (2oz) cheese, grated

Skate au gratin *(serves 4–6)*
POWER LEVEL: 100% (FULL)

1 Cut the skate wings into wedges and place in a large shallow dish. Pour over the milk, cover and cook for 7–8 min. Allow to stand for 5 min.
2 Drain off the milk from the skate and use to make 425ml (¾pt) béchamel sauce (page 112).
3 Skin the skate. Scatter half the cheese over the base of the dish, arrange the skate over the cheese and coat with the sauce. Sprinkle with the remaining cheese.
4 Cook, uncovered, for 3–4 min to heat through and melt the cheese on the top. Alternatively, brown under a hot grill.
5 Serve hot, garnished with glazed onions and triangles of fried or toasted bread.

For serving: triangles of fried or toasted bread and glazed onions (page 114)

Skate with caper butter (*serves 4–6*)   *colour page 11*
POWER LEVEL: 100% (FULL)

2 wings of skate, about 450g (1lb) each
50–75g (2–3oz) butter
1 × 15ml tbsp (1 tbsp) capers
5 × 15ml tbsp (5 tbsp) wine vinegar
1 × 15ml tbsp (1 tbsp) chopped parsley
salt and pepper

1 Cut each skate wing into 3 wedges. Place in a large shallow dish, cover with clingfilm, and cook for 5 min.
2 Melt and cook the butter for 5 min. Add the capers, vinegar, parsley and seasoning and cook for 2 min.
3 Skin the skate and lay the pieces in the serving dish. Pour the caper butter over the fish, cover and reheat for 3–4 min.
4 Serve hot.

Skate with orange (*serves 4–6*)
POWER LEVEL: 100% (FULL)

900g (2lb) skate
few drops lemon juice
25g (1oz) butter
1 onion, finely chopped
2 oranges
1 × 5ml tsp (1tsp) sugar
1 × 5ml tsp (1tsp) each chopped parsley and thyme
salt and pepper
few drops wine vinegar

1 Cut the skate wings into wedges. Place in a large shallow dish, sprinkle with lemon juice, cover and cook for 6 min. Allow to stand, and keep warm.
2 Melt half the butter in a bowl for 30 sec, add the onion, cover and cook for 3–4 min until soft.
3 Squeeze one of the oranges to extract the juice. Peel the other orange and cut into slices, removing any pips. Place the orange rounds in the bowl with the onions, add the sugar, juice from the other orange, herbs, seasoning and vinegar. Cover and cook until boiling.
4 Skin the pieces of skate and rearrange in the dish. Pour over the orange mixture, cover and cook for 2–3 min.
5 Serve immediately.

Sole

2 sole, filleted
3 slices onion
50g (2oz) button mushrooms
few sprigs parsley
1 bay leaf
salt and pepper
150ml (¼pt) dry white wine
150ml (¼pt) water
100g (4oz) white grapes
25g (1oz) butter
25g (1oz) plain flour
150ml (¼pt) milk,
  approximately
squeeze of lemon juice
2 × 15ml tbsp (2tbsp) single
  cream

Sole véronique (serves 4)   *colour opposite*
POWER LEVEL: 100% (FULL)

1   Trim the sole fillets, wash, wipe and lay them in a large shallow dish. Add the onion, sliced mushrooms, herbs, seasoning, wine and water. Cover and cook for 5 min. Drain off and reserve the stock.
2   Place the grapes in hot water for a few minutes, then peel, halve and remove pips, reserving a few halves for decoration.
3   Melt the butter in a large bowl for about 1 min. Stir in the flour and the fish stock, made up to 275ml (½pt) with the milk. Cook in the microwave for 3–4 min, stirring every minute.
4   Stir in the grapes, lemon juice and cream and pour the sauce over the fish. Reheat in the microwave for 3 min, then decorate with the reserved grapes and serve.

4 sole, skinned and filleted
salt and pepper
few drops lemon juice
16 peeled scampi, or canned or
  frozen mussels, thawed
275ml (½pt) béchamel sauce
  (page 112)
100g (4oz) gruyère or
  emmenthal cheese, grated
3–4 × 15ml tbsp (3–4tbsp)
  double cream
1–2 × 15ml tbsp (1–2tbsp)
  grated parmesan cheese
paprika for sprinkling

Paupiettes of sole in cheese sauce (serves 4–6)
POWER LEVEL: 100% (FULL)

1   Wipe or wash the sole fillets and dry. Sprinkle with salt and pepper and a few drops of lemon juice.
2   Place a scampi or mussel on each fillet and roll up like a swiss roll. Arrange the paupiettes in a circle on a plate, ensuring that the ends of the fillets are tucked underneath.
3   Cover and cook for 5–6 min. Leave to stand, arrange in a serving dish and keep warm.
4   Heat the béchamel sauce if necessary and stir in ¾ of the gruyère or emmenthal cheese. Mix well until smooth, then stir in the cream.
5   Spoon the sauce over the fish, sprinkle with the rest of the cheese and the grated parmesan.
6   Cook, uncovered, for 2–3 min until the cheese is melted; alternatively, brown under a hot grill. Sprinkle with paprika before serving.

2 medium sole, skinned and
  filleted
few drops lemon juice
4 large tomatoes, skinned
4 × 15ml tbsp (4tbsp) olive oil
2 × 15ml tbsp (2tbsp) wine
  vinegar
150ml (¼pt) tomato sauce
  (page 112)
1 × 15ml tbsp (1tbsp) mixed
  chopped herbs, ie parsley,
  chives, thyme

Sole andalouse (serves 4)   *colour page 107*
POWER LEVEL: 100% (FULL)

Serve as a starter or a cold fish course

1   Wipe the fish and fold each fillet in half. Place in a circle on a plate and sprinkle with lemon juice. Cover and cook for 2½–3 min, turning the plate once halfway through if necessary. Leave to cool.
2   Cut the tomatoes in half, arrange in a circle on a plate, cover and cook for 2 min, turning the plate halfway through. Leave to cool.
3   Blend the oil, vinegar and tomato sauce in a liquidiser or food processor. Stir in the herbs.
4   Drain the fish fillets. Place one on each of the tomato halves and coat with the dressing.
5   Garnish with anchovy fillets and watercress before serving cold.

DO NOT FREEZE

For garnish: anchovy fillets and watercress

*Sole Véronique (above); Brill with
Buttered Cucumber (page 24)*

2 medium sole or plaice
1 × 5ml tsp (1tsp) ground
   coriander
2 × 5ml tsp (2tsp) ground
   cumin
2 cloves garlic, crushed
1 small onion, grated
1.25cm (½in) fresh root ginger,
   grated *or* ½ × 5ml tsp
   (½tsp) ground ginger
1 × 5ml tsp (1tsp) turmeric
salt to taste
water to mix
red food colouring (optional)
40g (1½oz) butter, melted

Spiced sole *(serves 2)*   *colour page 23*
POWER LEVEL: 100% (FULL)

Plaice may be used instead of sole for this Indian dish. The fish is left to marinate in the spices before cooking.

1   Clean, skin and wash the fish. Make diagonal cuts crossways, 2.5–3.75cm (1–1½in) apart, on each side of the fish.
2   Combine the next 7 ingredients and add sufficient water to mix into a paste. Add a little red food colouring if required.
3   Rub the paste onto the outside of the fish and between the cuts; leave to marinate for 1¼–1½ hr.
4   Melt the butter in a large shallow dish for 1½ min. Place the fish in the dish and brush the butter over the top.
5   Cook, uncovered, for 6–7 min. Cover and stand for 5 min.
6   Sprinkle with caraway seeds and arrange on a bed of lettuce. Garnish with lemon slices before serving.

For garnish: ½ × 5ml tsp (½tsp) caraway seeds, lettuce leaves and lemon slices

8 fillets of sole or plaice
1 shallot or small onion, finely
   chopped
1 bay leaf
few sprigs parsley
150ml (¼pt) white wine
150ml (¼pt) water
salt and freshly ground black
   pepper
25g (1oz) butter
3 × 15ml tbsp (3tbsp) flour
3 × 15ml tbsp (3tbsp) single
   cream
2 tomatoes, skinned
1 × 15ml tbsp (1tbsp) chopped
   parsley

Fillets of sole duglère *(serves 4)*
POWER LEVEL: 100% (FULL)

1   Wash and dry the fish and place in a casserole dish with the shallot or onion, herbs, wine, water and seasoning. Cover and cook for 5–6 min. Drain off and reserve the liquid and keep the fish warm.
2   Melt the butter in a bowl or jug for 1 min, stir in the flour until smooth and gradually add the reserved fish liquid. Cook for 3–4 min until thickened, stirring every 30 sec. Stir in the cream.
3   Quarter the tomatoes and remove the seeds. Cut the flesh into dice and stir into the sauce with the parsley. Adjust seasoning and pour over the fish.
4   Heat through for 1–1½ min before serving.

Squid

Casserole of squid (*serves 4*)
POWER LEVEL: 100% (FULL) AND 30%

1 Peel the skin from the body of the squid; pull off the head and the entrails will follow. Take out the transparent backbone from the body and cut the tentacles from the head. The head, bone and innards are discarded.
2 Slice the body into thin rings, cut the tentacles, wash well in cold water and drain.
3 Cook the onion in the oil for 3–4 min. Add the squid, toss well, cover and cook for 2 min.
4 Stir in the tomato sauce, ¾ of the stock, bay leaf and seasoning. Reduce to 30% setting and cook, covered, for 30–35 min, stirring 3 times and adding the rest of the stock as required. Allow to stand for 10 min.
5 Sprinkle with chopped parsley and serve with boiled potatoes or rice.

For garnish: chopped fresh parsley
For serving: boiled potatoes or rice (page 114)

900g (2lb) squid
1 small onion, sliced
2 × 15ml tbsp (2tbsp) olive oil
275ml (½pt) tomato sauce (page 112)
150ml (¼pt) boiling chicken stock, approximately
1 bay leaf
salt and freshly ground black pepper

Squid with mushrooms (*serves 3–4*)   *colour page 92*
POWER LEVEL: 100% (FULL)

1 Clean the squid, discarding the head, skin, innards and transparent backbone. Cut into thin slices and place in a casserole dish with 2 × 15ml tbsp (2tbsp) of the oil.
2 Cover and cook for 4 min, stirring frequently throughout. Season to taste and add the sherry; leave to stand for 5 min.
3 Place the remaining 2 × 15ml tbsp (2tbsp) of the oil in a small bowl with the onions and mushrooms. Cover and cook for 3–4 min, stirring twice throughout. Add to the squid and mix together well.
4 Serve hot, garnished with watercress.

For garnish: watercress

450g (1lb) squid
4 × 15ml tbsp (4tbsp) oil
salt and freshly ground black pepper
2 × 15ml tbsp (2tbsp) dry sherry
5 spring onions, trimmed and sliced
225g (8oz) button mushrooms, sliced

Trout

Trout and almonds (*serves 4*)
POWER LEVEL: 100% (FULL)

1 Clean the fish, leaving the heads on. Wash and dry. Place in the serving dish, season lightly and add a few drops of lemon juice.
2 Melt the butter in the microwave for 2 min. Brush the trout with the butter, cover with kitchen paper and cook for 6–7 min.
3 Sprinkle almonds over the fish and cook for a further 2–4 min, depending on the size of the fish. Larger fish will take 1–2 min longer.
4 Serve hot with lemon wedges.

For serving: lemon wedges

4 trout, 225g (8oz) each, approximately
salt and pepper
few drops of lemon juice
50g (2oz) butter
50–75g (2–3oz) flaked almonds, toasted

15g (½oz) butter
1 shallot, finely chopped
4 trout, 900g (2lb),
   approximately, cleaned
150ml (¼pt) dry white wine
1 lemon, juice
2 × 15ml tbsp (2tbsp) chopped
   parsley
salt and freshly ground black
   pepper
150ml (¼pt) double cream
2–3 × 15ml tbsp (2–3tbsp)
   browned breadcrumbs

Baked trout with wine and cream *(serves 4)*
POWER LEVEL: 100% (FULL)

1 Melt the butter in a shallow casserole dish for 30 sec. Sprinkle in the shallot and add the trout, laying them in the dish head-to-tail. Brush with the butter.
2 Add the wine and lemon juice to the dish, sprinkle with the parsley and seasoning.
3 Cover and cook for 8–10 min, rearranging the trout—centre ones to the outside—if necessary halfway through. The cooking time will depend on the size of the trout; large fish will take 1–2 min longer.
4 Heat the cream for 30–45 sec and pour over the fish. Sprinkle with the browned breadcrumbs and serve immediately.

DO NOT FREEZE

3 smoked trout
1 lemon, juice
¼ × 5ml tsp (¼tsp) cayenne
   pepper
ground black pepper
75g (3oz) cream cheese
25g (1oz) butter

Smoked trout pâté *(serves 6)*
POWER LEVEL: 100% (FULL)

1 Remove the skin and bones from the trout, flake the fish and place in a bowl with the lemon juice, cayenne and black pepper to taste. Mash with a spoon or blend until smooth.
2 Cream the cheese lightly and add to the fish. Melt the butter for 1 min, add to the mixture and mix well together. Alternatively, purée together in a blender or food processor.
3 Place in a serving dish or individual dishes and chill.
4 Garnish with chopped parsley and serve with fingers of brown toast.

For garnish: 2 × 5ml tsp (2tsp) chopped parsley
For serving: fingers of brown toast

4 trout, 1.2 (2½lb),
   approximately
seasoned flour
50g (2oz) butter,
   approximately, softened
225g (8oz) small button
   mushrooms
1 clove garlic, crushed
3 × 15ml tbsp (3tbsp) pernod
   or dry sherry
150ml (¼pt) double cream
salt and freshly ground black
   pepper

Trout with mushrooms *(serves 4)*   *colour opposite*
POWER LEVEL: 100% (FULL)

The trout are cooked in a browning dish

1 Clean the trout and remove the heads. Rinse in cold water and dry. Coat each trout in seasoned flour, pressing well into the skin of the fish.
2 Pre-heat a browning dish for 6–8 min, depending on its size, add about half the butter and if necessary heat for a further 30 sec.
3 Quickly add 2 of the trout, pressing the fish against the base of the dish with a heatproof spatula. Cover and cook for 1½–2 min; turn the trout over and cook for a further 1½–2 min.
4 Remove the trout, pre-heat the dish for another 2–3 min and cook the remaining trout as before, using a little more butter if required. Remove the trout and keep warm. Drain off the juices from the dish.
5 Wipe the mushrooms and stir into the dish with the garlic and pernod or sherry. Cook, uncovered, for 4 min until the mushrooms are tender.
6 Stir in the cream and heat through for 30–45 sec. Season to taste and pour the sauce over the trout.
7 Serve immediately with boiled buttered new potatoes and a green salad.

For serving: boiled buttered new potatoes and green salad

Trout with Mushrooms (above)

Tuna

1 × 20cm (8in) baked flan case (page 116)

For the filling:

25g (1oz) butter or margarine
1 small onion, peeled and finely chopped
75ml (2½fl oz) milk
200g (7oz) can sweetcorn
198g (7oz) can tuna fish, drained and flaked
2 eggs, beaten
salt and freshly ground black pepper
75g (3oz) cheese, finely grated

Sweetcorn and tuna flan *(serves 6)*
POWER LEVEL: 100% (FULL) AND 50% (DEFROST)

1 Melt the butter or margarine in a large bowl for 1 min, add the onion, toss well, cover and cook for 3 min until soft.
2 Add the milk and contents of the can of sweetcorn with the tuna fish. Beat in the eggs and the seasoning. Stir in half the cheese.
3 Pour into the flan case and sprinkle with the remaining cheese.
4 Cook on 50% (defrost) setting for 14–16 min, turning every 3 min. Leave to stand for 10–15 min.
5 Serve hot or cold with a green salad.

For serving: green salad

300g (10oz) canned tuna fish, drained
2 × 15ml tbsp (2tbsp) lemon juice
150ml (¼pt) milk
175g (6oz) breadcrumbs, fresh white or brown
2 eggs, beaten
1 medium onion, grated
salt and freshly ground black pepper
1 × 15ml tbsp (1tbsp) dried parsley

Tuna fish mould *(serves 4–6)*
POWER LEVEL: 70%

1 Pound or mince the tuna fish, or put through a food processor, and mix with the rest of the ingredients.
2 Pour into a lightly greased microwave ring mould and cook, covered, for 15–18 min. Stand for 20 min, then turn out of the ring mould.
3 Serve warm or cold with a salad of watercress and sliced button mushrooms tossed in a french or vinaigrette dressing (page 109).

For serving: watercress and mushroom salad (see method 3)

675g (1½lb) potatoes, washed
2 × 15ml tbsp (2tbsp) oil
1 large onion, peeled and sliced
1 clove garlic, crushed
425g (15oz) can tomatoes
1 × 5ml tsp (1tsp) dried mixed herbs
salt and freshly ground black pepper
198g (7oz) can tuna fish, drained and flaked
75g (3oz) cheddar cheese, grated

Potato and tuna bake *(serves 4)*
POWER LEVEL: 100% (FULL) AND 50% (DEFROST)

1 Prick the skins of the potatoes with a fork and cook in the microwave for 10–12 min.
2 Carefully remove the skins and dice the potato.
3 Place the oil in a large bowl, toss in the onion and garlic, cover and cook for 5–6 min. Stir in the tomatoes, herbs and seasoning to taste.
4 Layer the potato, tuna fish and tomato mixture in a 20cm (8in) round casserole, starting with a layer of potato and ending with a layer of tomato.
5 Cover and cook for 5 min, then reduce to 50% (defrost) setting for 15–20 min until the potatoes are tender. Allow to stand for 5 min.
6 Sprinkle with the grated cheese, cook on 100% (full) setting for 2–3 min to melt the cheese. Alternatively, brown under a hot grill.
7 Serve hot with crusty french bread or garlic bread.

For serving: crusty french bread or garlic bread

Thatched tuna pie (*serves 4–6*)
POWER LEVEL: 100% (FULL)

1 Melt the butter or margarine in a large round shallow dish for 1 min, toss in the leeks, cover and cook for 3–4 min. Add the sauce and tomatoes.
2 Drain and flake the tuna and add to the sauce with the parsley, lemon rind and juice and seasoning. Mix together well, smooth the top and clean the edges of the dish.
3 Mix the breadcrumbs with the grated cheese and sprinkle over the top of the sauce mixture. Sprinkle with a little grated nutmeg.
4 Cook for 6 min, turning every 2 min, until heated through.
5 Serve hot, garnished with parsley sprigs.

For garnish: parsley sprigs

25g (1oz) butter or margarine
2 medium leeks, trimmed and finely sliced
275ml (½pt) béchamel sauce (page 112)
4 tomatoes, skinned and quartered
450g (1lb) canned tuna fish, approximately
1 × 15ml tbsp (1tbsp) chopped parsley
½ lemon, grated rind and juice
salt and freshly ground black pepper
50g (2oz) fresh brown breadcrumbs
50g (2oz) red leicester cheese, finely grated
grated nutmeg for sprinkling

Turbot

Turbot en coquille (*serves 6*)   *colour on cover*
POWER LEVEL: 100% (FULL)

Six deep scallop shells are required for serving, but if these are not available, small individual dishes can be used instead. Cod or other firm-fleshed fish may be used as an alternative to the turbot if required

1 Wash the fish and dry. Sprinkle with lemon juice and seasoning.
2 Melt the butter in a casserole dish or on a large plate for 30 sec. Arrange the fish in the dish and brush with melted butter. Cover and cook for 6–7 min, turning the fish or rearranging the fish steaks halfway through if necessary. Drain the fish well and leave to stand and cool.
3 Place the cucumber in a bowl, sprinkle with a little salt and leave for 30 min to draw out the moisture. Drain well and sprinkle with black pepper, herbs and wine.
4 Whisk the boiling water into the mayonnaise. Arrange the lettuce leaves in the base of the shells or individual dishes and top with the cucumber.
5 When the fish is cold, remove the skin and bones and flake the flesh with a fork. Divide between the shells and spoon the mayonnaise over the top.
6 Cut the anchovy fillets into halves lengthways and use to garnish each shell before serving decorated with a little lumpfish caviar.

For garnish: 50g (2oz) can anchovy fillets, drained, a little lumpfish caviar (optional)

675g (1½lb) turbot steaks
½ lemon, juice
salt and freshly ground black pepper
15g (½oz) butter
½ cucumber, peeled and diced
1 × 5ml tsp (1tsp) chopped fresh mixed herbs
few drops white wine vinegar
1 × 15ml tbsp (1tbsp) boiling water
150ml (¼pt) thick mayonnaise (page 108)
lettuce leaves

Turbot with crab sauce *(serves 4)*
POWER LEVEL: 100% (FULL)

1 Wash and dry the fish, place in a shallow casserole dish with the lemon juice, seasoning, parsley, bay leaf and wine. Cover and cook for 8–9 min until tender. Drain off, reserve and measure the stock.
2 Melt the butter in a bowl for 1 min and stir in the flour. Make the liquid quantity of the reserved stock up to 275ml (½pt) with the milk and gradually stir this into the butter and flour. Cook for 3–4 min until cooked and thickened, stirring every 30 sec.
3 Stir in the crabmeat and cook for a further 1–2 min. Remove bay leaf, adjust seasoning and spoon the sauce over the turbot.
4 Sprinkle with parmesan cheese and paprika and heat through, uncovered, for 1–2 min; alternatively, brown under a hot grill.
5 Garnish with a few parsley sprigs and serve hot.

For garnish: parsley sprigs

4 turbot or halibut steaks, 675g (1½lb), approximately
few drops lemon juice
salt and pepper
few parsley sprigs
1 bay leaf
150ml (¼pt) white wine
25g (1oz) butter
25g (1oz) flour
150ml (¼pt) milk, approximately
75–100g (3–4oz) canned crabmeat, flaked
25g (1oz) parmesan cheese, grated
paprika for sprinkling

Turbot with sweetcorn *(serves 4)* colour page 61
POWER LEVEL: 100% (FULL)

1 Wipe and trim the fish steaks.
2 Melt half the butter in a shallow dish for 1 min, add the fish and coat well in the butter. Sprinkle with the seasoning and lemon juice.
3 Cover and cook for 6–7 min, turning the dish or rearranging the fish halfway through if necessary. Drain off the liquor and keep the fish warm.
4 Heat the sweetcorn in a covered bowl for 3–4 min and stir in the rest of the butter. Make the hollandaise sauce.
5 Arrange the sweetcorn in the base of a serving dish and arrange the fish steaks on top.
6 Coat with the hollandaise sauce and garnish with parsley and lemon twists. Serve immediately with freshly cooked broccoli spears.

For garnish: chopped parsley and lemon twists
For serving: broccoli spears

4 turbot or halibut steaks, 675g (1½lb), approximately
75g (3oz) unsalted butter
salt and freshly ground black pepper
few drops lemon juice
425g (15oz) can sweetcorn
hollandaise sauce (page 109)

Whiting

Whiting mornay *(serves 4)*
POWER LEVEL: 100% (FULL)

1 Place the fish, milk and butter in a casserole dish, cover and cook for 3 min. Remove the fish, take off the skin and flake the flesh.
2 Add the eggs, tomatoes and parsley sauce to the dish. Mix together well and stir in the fish and season to taste. Smooth the top and wipe the sides of the dish.
3 Mix together the cheese and breadcrumbs and sprinkle over the fish mixture. Cook, uncovered, for 1–2 min until the cheese has melted. Alternatively, brown the top under a hot grill.
4 Garnish with the olives and watercress before serving.

For garnish: stuffed olives and watercress

350g (12oz) whiting fillets
2 × 15ml tbsp (2tbsp) milk
15g (½oz) butter
2 hard-boiled eggs, chopped
3 tomatoes, skinned and sliced
425ml (¾pt) parsley sauce (page 109)
salt and freshly ground black pepper
50g (2oz) cheese, grated
25g (1oz) browned breadcrumbs

Crab and Sweetcorn Soup (page 32); Squid with Mushrooms (page 87)

93

50g (2oz) butter
1 small onion, finely sliced
350–450g (¾–1lb) green
    cabbage, finely shredded
salt and pepper
675g (1½lb) whiting fillets
few drops lemon juice
275ml (½pt) cheese sauce
    (page 109)
1 × 15ml tbsp (1tbsp) parmesan
    cheese
paprika for sprinkling

Whiting with cabbage (*serves 4–5*)
POWER LEVEL: 100% (FULL)

1   Melt the butter in a large casserole dish for 1½ min, stir in the onion, cover and cook for 3 min. Add the cabbage and seasonings. Mix together well, cover and cook for 8–10 min until tender, stirring 2–3 times throughout. Leave to stand.
2   Sprinkle the fish with seasoning and a few drops of lemon juice. Fold over the fillets, place in a dish or on a plate, cover and cook for 6–7 min.
3   Drain and place the fish on top of the cabbage. Heat the cheese sauce if necessary and spoon over the fish and cabbage.
4   Sprinkle with parmesan cheese and paprika and heat through, uncovered, for 2–3 min. Alternatively, brown under a hot grill.

25g (1oz) butter
8 whiting fillets
salt and paprika
1 lemon, juice
1 orange, grated rind and juice
150ml (¼pt) double cream
1 wine glass dry white wine
2 egg yolks
pinch cayenne pepper

Whiting with orange sauce (*serves 4*)   *colour page 77*
POWER LEVEL: 100% (FULL) AND 50% (DEFROST)

1   Melt the butter in a large shallow casserole dish for 1 min. Overlap the whiting fillets in the dish and brush with the melted butter. Sprinkle with salt and paprika and half the lemon juice. Cover and cook for 5–6 min, turning or rearranging the fillets halfway through. Leave to stand.
2   Mix together in a bowl the remaining lemon juice, orange rind and juice, cream, wine and egg yolks. Beat well and cook on 50% (defrost) setting for 5–6 min until thickened, whisking every 30 sec. Do not allow to boil. Season to taste with salt and cayenne pepper.
3   Drain the fish fillets and place on a serving platter. Spoon some of the sauce over the fish and hand the rest separately.
4   Sprinkle with chopped parsley and arrange the orange wedges around the fish.

DO NOT FREEZE

For garnish: orange wedges and chopped parsley

Salad Niçoise (page 18);
Bouillabaise (page 102);
Moules à la Marinière (page 55)

94

General fish recipes

I have included recipes in this section which require a selection or combination of various sorts of fish, or when the type of fish required for the main ingredient can be chosen according to preference.

900g (2lb) potatoes, cooked and mashed
25g (1oz) butter
2 × 15ml tbsp (2tbsp) milk
40g (1½oz) butter
1 small onion, sliced
40g (1½oz) flour
425ml (¾pt) milk
salt and freshly ground black pepper
350g (12oz) cooked fish, flaked
100g (4oz) peeled prawns, fresh, canned or frozen, thawed
100g (4oz) cheese, grated
paprika for sprinkling

Fisherman's pie *(serves 4–6)*
POWER LEVEL: 100% (FULL) AND 70%

1 If the potatoes are cold, heat them in the microwave for about 3 min. Beat in 25g (1oz) butter and 2 × 15ml tbsp (2tbsp) milk.
2 Melt 40g (1½oz) butter for 1–1½ min, add the onion, toss well in the butter, cover and cook for 3 min. Stir in the flour, then gradually stir in 425ml (¾pt) milk. Cook for 4–4½ min until bubbling and thickened, stirring every minute.
3 Add seasoning, stir in the remaining ingredients and place the mixture in a pie dish. Put the creamed potato into a piping bag fitted with a large star nozzle and pipe swirls of potato over the top of the fish mixture.
4 Reduce to a 70% setting and heat the pie through, uncovered, for 4–5 min. Cover and allow to stand for 3–4 min.
5 Sprinkle with paprika; alternatively, brown under a hot grill.

175g (6oz) green lasagne
1 litre (1¾pt) boiling water
1 × 15ml tbsp (1tbsp) oil
1 × 5ml tsp (1tsp) salt
50g (2oz) butter or margarine
1 small onion, finely chopped
50g (2oz) flour
550ml (1pt) milk
450g (1lb) smoked fish fillet, ie cod or haddock
200g (7oz) can sweetcorn
freshly ground black pepper
100g (4oz) peeled prawns
salt (optional)
50g (2oz) cheddar cheese, grated
paprika for sprinkling

Smoked fish and prawn lasagne *(serves 4–6)*   *colour page 81*
POWER LEVEL: 100% (FULL)

1 Place the lasagne leaves in a large oblong dish. Add boiling water, oil and salt. Cover and cook for 10 min. Separate the leaves of pasta with a spoon and, if not quite done, continue to cook for a further 2–3 min. Allow to stand for a few minutes.
2 Drain the lasagne and pat dry with kitchen paper.
3 Melt the butter or margarine in a large bowl or jug for 1–1½ min, add the onion, cover and cook for 3–3½ min until tender. Stir in the flour and gradually add the milk.
4 Cut the fish into small bite-size pieces and add to the sauce with the sweetcorn and black pepper.
5 Cover and cook in the microwave for about 9–10 min until cooked and thickened, stirring every 3 min. Add the prawns and cook for a further 2 min. Adjust seasoning.
6 Layer sauce and lasagne in the oblong dish, beginning and ending with the sauce. Sprinkle with the cheese.
7 Return to the microwave and cook for about 5 min until heated through and the cheese is melted.
8 Sprinkle with paprika and serve hot.

Seafood pancakes (*serves 4 or 8*)
POWER LEVEL: 100% (FULL)

1 Add the sweetcorn and fish to the béchamel sauce. Stir in the cream.
2 Season to taste and add a few drops of lemon juice. Heat in the microwave for 3–4 min or until hot.
3 Divide the filling between the pancakes, then fold or roll up each one. Arrange on a serving dish or plate, dot with slivers of butter and sprinkle with the cheese.
4 Cover with clingfilm, making a slit with the pointed end of a sharp knife, and heat through for 2½–3½ min.
5 Remove clingfilm. Serve hot with lemon wedges and garnish with sprigs of parsley or watercress.

For garnish: sprigs of parsley or watercress
For serving: lemon wedges

3 × 15ml tbsp (3tbsp) sweetcorn kernels
350g (12oz) cooked fish or shellfish or a mixture of both
275ml (½pt) béchamel sauce (page 112)
3 × 15ml tbsp (3tbsp) thick cream
salt and freshly ground black pepper
few drops lemon juice
8 cooked pancakes (page 117)
slivers butter
4 × 15ml tbsp (4tbsp) grated cheese

Fish cakes (*serves 6*)
POWER LEVEL: 100% (FULL)

These fish cakes are cooked in a browning dish

1 Flake the fish, removing any skin and bones. Mash the potato and mix in together with the fish, ½ egg, lemon juice and rind, seasoning and parsley.
2 Turn the mixture onto a floured board or work surface and divide into 6 portions. Shape each portion into a flat round circle.
3 Dip each fish cake into the seasoned flour, then the beaten egg and finally coat with the breadcrumbs.
4 Pre-heat the browning dish for 6–8 min, depending on its size, add the oil and heat for a further minute.
5 Add the fish cakes to the browning dish, pressing each one down with a heatproof spatula. Cook for 2 min, turn the fish cakes over and cook for a further 2½–3 min. Drain on kitchen paper.
6 Serve hot with parsley sauce.

For serving: parsley sauce (page 109)

225g (8oz) cooked fish
100g (4oz) cooked potatoes
½ egg
½ lemon, juice and rind, finely grated
salt and pepper
1 × 5ml tsp (1tsp) chopped parsley
seasoned flour
1 egg, beaten
breadcrumbs, toasted
3 × 15ml tbsp (3tbsp) oil

Tomato fish crumble (*serves 4–6*)
POWER LEVEL: 100% (FULL)

1 Lightly grease a large round ovenware dish.
2 Mix the tomato sauce with the sliced mushrooms and fish. Place in the greased dish.
3 Sift the flours with the salt and mustard and rub in the butter or margarine until the mixture resembles fine crumbs. Stir in the grated cheese.
4 Sprinkle the crumble topping lightly over the tomato mixture and smooth the top.
5 Cook for 8–10 min, giving a quarter turn every 2 min until heated through and the crumble is cooked.
6 Serve hot, garnished with tomato slices.

For garnish: tomato slices

550ml (1pt) tomato sauce (page 112)
225g (8oz) mushrooms, washed and sliced
450g (1lb) cooked fish
75g (3oz) wholemeal flour
75g (3oz) plain flour
½ × 5ml tsp (½tsp) salt
½ × 5ml tsp (½tsp) dry mustard
75g (3oz) butter or margarine
75g (3oz) cheese, finely grated

Fish pudding (*serves 4–5*)
POWER LEVEL: 100% (FULL)

This pudding is very light in texture and makes a good lunch or supper dish

1 Lightly grease a 850ml (1½pt) pudding basin.
2 Flake the fish, discarding any skin or bones. Mix with the breadcrumbs, parsley, lemon rind and seasoning.
3 Melt the butter for 1–1½ min and add to the fish with the beaten eggs. Mix together well.
4 Place in the greased pudding basin. Cover with clingfilm, making a slit with the pointed end of a sharp knife.
5 Cook for 4–5 min, turning once halfway through.
6 Remove the clingfilm and invert onto the serving dish.
7 Serve hot with tomato sauce or cold with a dressed salad.

For serving: tomato sauce (page 112) or a dressed salad

450g (1lb) white fish fillets, cooked
75g (3oz) white breadcrumbs
1 × 15ml tbsp (1tbsp) chopped parsley
1 lemon, grated rind
salt and freshly ground black pepper
50g (2oz) butter or margarine
2 eggs, beaten

Mixed seafood casserole (*serves 4*)   *colour opposite*
POWER LEVEL: 100% (FULL) AND 70%

1 Cut the cod and huss into 5cm (2in) pieces and place in a casserole dish with the scallops. Sprinkle with a few drops of lemon juice, cover and cook for 2 min.
2 Mix the crabmeat with the sauce, add the dill and adjust seasoning to taste. Pour the sauce over the fish in the casserole dish. Cover and cook on 70% setting for 10–12 min.
3 Heat the creamed potato if necessary for 1–2 min on 100% (full) setting and beat in the tomato purée. Place in a piping bag fitted with a large star nozzle and pipe a border of potato around the edge of the dish.
4 Sprinkle the cheese in the centre and cook, uncovered, on 70% setting for approximately 4–5 min until heated through and the cheese is melted. Sprinkle with paprika; alternatively, brown the top under a hot grill.
5 Serve hot, garnished with prawns and parsley.

For garnish: few prawns and chopped parsley

225g (8oz) cod fillet, skinned
225g (8oz) huss
4 scallops
few drops lemon juice
100g (4oz) crabmeat
275ml (½pt) hot parsley sauce (page 109)
2 × 5ml tsp (2tsp) chopped fresh dill *or* ½ × 5ml tsp (½tsp) dried dill
salt and freshly ground black pepper
675g (1½lb) creamed potato (page 113)
2 × 15ml tbsp (2tbsp) tomato purée
50g (2oz) cheddar cheese, grated
paprika for sprinkling

Fish pie
POWER LEVEL: 100% (FULL)

1 Put the soup and milk into an ovenware dish. Heat for 1 min, stir, then heat for a further 2 min. Mix thoroughly.
2 Add the peas and cooked fish and pour into a 850ml (1½pt) pie dish. Cook for 4 min, stirring once during cooking.
3 Sprinkle half the crisps on top of the mixture, cover with the cheese and top with the remaining crisps.
4 Cook for 1½ min or until the cheese is melted. Sprinkle with chopped parsley and serve.

DO NOT FREEZE THE COMPLETE DISH—THE CRISP TOPPING SHOULD BE ADDED AFTER THAWING

For garnish: 1 × 15ml tbsp (1tbsp) chopped parsley

298g (10½oz) can condensed vegetable soup
150ml (¼pt) milk
3 × 15ml tbsp (3tbsp) frozen peas
450g (1lb) cooked fish
salt and pepper
75g (3oz) potato crisps
50g (2oz) cheddar cheese, grated

Mixed Seafood Casserole (above)

175g (6oz) shortcrust pastry
  (page 116)
225g (8oz) white fish, eg cod or
  haddock fillets
few drops lemon juice
25g (1oz) butter or margarine
1 medium onion, peeled and
  finely sliced
25g (1oz) flour
150ml (¼pt) milk
salt and pepper to taste
3 eggs, beaten
4 tomatoes, skinned
25–50g (1–2oz) cheese, finely
  grated
paprika for sprinkling

White fish flan (serves 6)
POWER LEVEL: 100% (FULL) AND 50% (DEFROST)

1 Roll out the pastry, line a 20cm (8in) flan dish and bake blind (page 116).
2 Put the fish into a dish or on a plate, sprinkle with lemon juice, cover and cook for 2–2½ min, turning once halfway through.
3 Drain the fish, reserving the juices. Flake the fish, discarding any bones or skin.
4 Melt the butter or margarine for 1 min in a bowl, add the onion, toss well and cook for 2–3 min until soft and transparent. Stir in the flour and gradually add the milk and reserved juices. Mix well and season to taste.
5 Cook for 2–3 min, stirring every minute until thickened. Leave to cool slightly before beating in the eggs.
6 Slice the tomatoes thinly and arrange with the fish in the bottom of the flan case. Season well.
7 Pour over the sauce, smooth the top and sprinkle with the grated cheese and paprika.
8 Cook for 4 min, giving a quarter turn every minute. Allow to stand for 5 min, then cook for a further 2 min. Alternatively, cook on 50% (defrost) setting for 14–16 min, turning every 3 min. If not quite set, heat for 15–30 sec periods or allow to stand after removal from the oven for 15–20 min.
9 Serve on its own as a snack, or with potatoes and a green vegetable as a main meal.

For serving: potatoes and a green vegetable

225g (8oz) fennel, trimmed
  and sliced
3 × 15ml tbsp (3tbsp) water
25g (1oz) butter
40g (1½oz) flour
425g (15oz) can cream of celery
  soup
675g (1½lb) white fish fillets,
  ie cod or haddock, skinned
salt and freshly ground black
  pepper
4 × 15ml tbsp (4tbsp) chopped
  parsley
2 × 5ml tsp (2tsp) lemon juice
450g (1lb) new potatoes,
  cooked and sliced
15g (½oz) butter, melted
paprika for sprinkling

Summer fish pie (serves 4)
POWER LEVEL: 100% (FULL) AND 70%

1 Place the fennel and water in a covered dish or boiling bag. Cook for 6–7 min until tender but still crisp, stirring once halfway through.
2 Melt 25g (1oz) butter in a large bowl or casserole dish for 1 min, stir in the flour and the soup.
3 Cut the fish into small bite-size pieces and add to the soup with the drained fennel and seasoning to taste.
4 Cover and bring to the boil in the microwave, about 4–5 min, until thickened, stirring every minute. Reduce to 70% setting and continue to cook for 6 min.
5 Add the parsley and lemon juice to the mixture and turn into a serving dish. Arrange the slices of potato over the top, brush with the melted butter and sprinkle with paprika.
6 Heat on 100% (full) setting, uncovered, for 2–3 min. Serve hot, garnished with chopped parsley.

For garnish: chopped parsley

Seafood pilaf (*serves 4–6*)
POWER LEVEL: 100% (FULL)

1 Melt 25g (1oz) butter for 1 min in a large casserole dish, stir in the onion, cover and cook for 3–4 min. Stir in the rice, cover and cook for 1 min.
2 Add about half the fish stock to the rice, stir well and add seasoning and turmeric. Cover and cook for about 12 min, adding extra stock as necessary and stirring 2–3 times throughout. Leave to stand.
3 Melt the remaining 25g (1oz) butter for 1 min, add the mushrooms, cover and cook for 1 min. Stir in the prawns, scampi and the mussels, cover and cook for 4–5 min. Leave to stand for 2 min.
4 Fork over the rice and stir in the melted butter. Add the mushroom and shellfish mixture. Serve hot, garnished with a few prawns in their shells and lemon wedges.

DO NOT FREEZE

For garnish: few prawns in their shells and lemon wedges

50g (2oz) butter
1 medium onion, finely chopped
225g (8oz) long grain rice
550ml (1pt) boiling chicken or fish stock (page 113)
salt and pepper
1 × 5ml tsp (1tsp) turmeric
100g (4oz) mushrooms, sliced
100g (4oz) peeled prawns, fresh or frozen, thawed
225g (8oz) peeled scampi, fresh or frozen, thawed
225g (8oz) mussels, canned or frozen, thawed
15g (½oz) butter, melted

Seafood pasta salad (*serves 4*)
POWER LEVEL: 100% (FULL)

1 Place water, salt and oil in a large bowl and heat in the microwave for 4 min. Add the pasta and cook for 10 min. Stir well, then drain and rinse with cold water.
2 Return the pasta to a serving bowl and stir in the remaining ingredients except the vinaigrette dressing.
3 Finally, add the dressing to the salad and toss lightly before serving.

DO NOT FREEZE

550ml (1pt) boiling water
1 × 5ml tsp (1tsp) salt
1 × 15ml tbsp (1tbsp) oil
175g (6oz) shell pasta
100g (4oz) frozen mussels, thawed
198g (7oz) can tuna fish
225g (8oz) tomatoes, skinned and chopped
1 green pepper, finely chopped
425g (15oz) can kidney beans, drained and rinsed
salt and freshly ground black pepper
vinaigrette dressing (page 109)

2–3 × 15ml tbsp (2–3tbsp) oil
2 sticks celery, finely sliced
1 onion, chopped
1 green pepper, deseeded and
 diced
1 clove garlic, crushed
1 × 15ml tbsp (1tbsp)
 worcestershire sauce
425g (15oz) can tomatoes
275ml (½pt) tomato juice
salt and freshly ground black
 pepper
100g (4oz) long grain rice
175g (6oz) okra, trimmed and
 sliced
275g (10oz) peeled prawns,
 fresh or frozen, thawed
275g (10oz) crab or lobster
 meat, fresh or frozen, thawed
4 × 15ml tbsp (4tbsp) dry
 sherry

Seafood gumbo with rice *(serves 6)*   *colour opposite*
POWER LEVEL: 100% (FULL) AND 70%

1 Mix together the oil, celery, onion and green pepper in a large bowl or
   casserole dish. Cover and cook for 5–6 min.
2 Add garlic, worcestershire sauce, tomatoes, tomato juice, seasoning, rice
   and okra. Stir well, cover and bring to the boil in the microwave, about
   5 min. Reduce to 70% setting and continue to cook for 15 min.
3 Stir in the prawns and crab or lobster meat and the sherry. Cover and cook
   for a further 5 min.
4 Allow to stand for 10 min before serving with garlic or herb bread.

For serving: garlic or herb bread (pages 114 and 116)

2 × 15ml tbsp (2tbsp) oil
1 small onion, finely chopped
75g (3oz) leek, finely chopped
2–3 cloves garlic, crushed
225g (8oz) can tomatoes
850ml (1½pt) boiling fish stock
 (page 113)
1 × 15ml tbsp (1tbsp) tomato
 purée
salt and freshly ground black
 pepper
2 × 15ml tbsp (2tbsp) chopped
 mixed fresh herbs, ie parsley,
 thyme, basil
1 bay leaf
450g (1lb) prepared mixed fresh
 fish, cut into small pieces
225g (8oz) peeled prawns
225g (8oz) frozen mussels,
 thawed

Bouillabaise *(serves 6)*   *colour page 95*
POWER LEVEL: 100% (FULL)

*The flavour of the soup is made more interesting if as many varieties of fish as
possible are included. Use the trimmings from the fish to make the stock*

1 Place the oil, onion, leek and garlic in a large casserole dish, cover and
   cook for 3–4 min until the onion and leek are transparent.
2 Add all the other ingredients except the prawns and mussels. Stir well,
   cover and bring to the boil and continue to cook for 6–7 min.
3 Stir in the prawns and mussels and cook for a further 2–3 min. Adjust
   seasoning and allow to stand for a few minutes.
4 Remove the bay leaf and serve hot with crusty french bread.

For serving: crusty french bread

*Hot Seafood Dip (page 104);
Seafood Gumbo with Rice (above)*

2–3 × 15ml tbsp (2–3tbsp) oil
1 large onion, finely chopped
1 green pepper, deseeded and
  finely chopped
1 clove garlic, finely chopped
150ml (¼pt) dry white wine
425g (15oz) can tomatoes
½ × 5ml tsp (½tsp) thyme
¼ × 5ml tsp (¼tsp) oregano or
  basil
1 bay leaf
¼ × 5ml tsp (¼tsp) tabasco
  sauce
225g (8oz) long grain rice
salt and freshly ground black
  pepper
225g (8oz) peeled prawns
225g (8oz) cooked ham or
  sausage, diced

Quick jambalaya *(serves 6)*
POWER LEVEL: 100% (FULL) AND 70%

1 Mix together the oil, onion, pepper and garlic in a large bowl or casserole dish. Cover and cook for 5–6 min until tender.
2 Add the wine, tomatoes, herbs, bay leaf, tabasco sauce and the rice. Season to taste, cover and cook for 5 min.
3 Reduce to 70% setting and cook for a further 15 min. Add the prawns and ham or sausage, continue to cook for another 5 min, adding more liquid if necessary.
4 Allow to stand for 10 min. Remove the bay leaf before garnishing with chopped parsley. Serve hot.

For garnish: 2 × 15ml tbsp (2tbsp) chopped parsley

50g (2oz) butter
1 small onion, finely sliced
1 red pepper, deseeded and cut
  into thin strips
450g (1lb) white cabbage, finely
  shredded
salt and freshly ground black
  pepper
1 × 5ml tsp (1tsp) dried thyme
275ml (½pt) cider
2 × 15ml tbsp (2tbsp) tomato
  purée
450g (1lb) white fish fillets,
  skinned
100g (4oz) frozen peas, thawed

Fisherman's slaw *(serves 4)*   *colour page 37*
POWER LEVEL: 100% (FULL)

1 Melt the butter in a large casserole dish or bowl for 2 min. Add the onion and pepper, cover and cook for 4 min.
2 Stir in the cabbage, seasoning, thyme, cider and tomato purée. Cover and cook for 10–11 min until the cabbage is just cooked but still slightly crisp.
3 Cut the fish into 5cm (2in) pieces and add to the casserole with the peas. Cover and cook for 4–5 min. Allow to stand for 5 min before serving.

225g (8oz) crabmeat, canned or
  frozen, thawed
175g (6oz) peeled prawns
2 × 400g (14oz) cans lobster or
  prawn bisque
1 × 15ml tbsp (1tbsp) chopped
  basil *or* ¼ × 5ml tsp (¼tsp)
  dried basil
salt and freshly ground black
  pepper

Hot seafood dip *(serves 10–12)*   *colour page 103*
POWER LEVEL: 100% (FULL)

Serve as a starter or part of a buffet menu

1 Flake the crabmeat and chop the peeled prawns.
2 Mix together with the lobster or prawn bisque, herbs and seasoning.
3 Cover and cook for 6–8 min until heated through, stirring twice throughout.
4 Serve hot with bite-size chunks of french bread for dipping.

For serving: french bread

Curried seafood ring (*serves 6*)
POWER LEVEL: 100% (FULL)

1 Place the rice, onion and pepper in a large bowl. Stir in the turmeric, boiling water, oil and seasoning.
2 Cook for 10–12 min until the rice is tender. Allow to stand for 5 min.
3 Drain off any excess water, then press the rice firmly into a lightly greased ring mould. Leave to cool, then chill in the refrigerator.
4 Flake the fish and mix with the prawns. Blend together the mayonnaise and curry paste and stir into the fish mixture.
5 When the rice mould is firm and cold, turn out onto a serving plate. Pile the fish mixture into the centre and sprinkle with paprika.
6 Serve cold, garnished with lemon twists and a few prawns.

DO NOT FREEZE

For garnish: lemon twists and a few prawns

225g (8oz) long grain, easy-cook rice
1 small onion, finely chopped
1 green pepper, deseeded and finely chopped
1 × 5ml tsp (1tsp) turmeric
550ml (1pt) boiling water
1 × 15ml tbsp (1tbsp) oil
salt and freshly ground black pepper
350g (12oz) white fish fillets, cooked
100g (4oz) peeled prawns
4 × 15ml tbsp (4tbsp) mayonnaise
1 × 5ml tsp (1tsp) curry paste
paprika for sprinkling

Fish chowder (*serves 4*)
POWER LEVEL: 100% (FULL)

1 Mix together the oil, bacon, onion and celery in a large casserole dish, cover and cook for 2 min.
2 Add the potatoes, mix together well, cover and cook for 11–12 min, stirring twice throughout.
3 Add the fish, stock, turmeric, thyme, bay leaf and seasonings. Cover and cook for 5–6 min.
4 Adjust seasoning and add the clams or mussels. Cover and heat through for 2 min. Remove bay leaf.
5 Stir in the single cream and 1 × 15ml tbsp (1tbsp) chopped parsley. Sprinkle with the rest of the parsley and serve hot with crusty bread or herb bread.

For garnish: 2 × 15ml tbsp (2tbsp) chopped parsley
For serving: crusty bread or herb bread (page 116)

1 × 15ml tbsp (1tbsp) cooking oil
2 bacon rashers, derinded and chopped
1 medium onion, chopped
2 sticks celery, chopped
350g (12oz) potatoes, cut into small dice
350g (12oz) white fish fillets, cut into 2.5cm (2in) pieces
550ml (1pt) boiling chicken or fish stock (page 113)
¼ × 5ml tsp (¼tsp) turmeric
¼ × 5ml tsp (¼tsp) dried thyme
1 bay leaf
salt and freshly ground black pepper
275g (10oz) can or jar baby clams or mussels, drained
150ml (¼pt) single cream

105

6 chicken thigh joints

2 × 15ml tbsp (2tbsp) oil

1 spanish onion, finely chopped

2–3 cloves garlic, finely
  chopped

225g (8oz) long grain,
  easy-cook rice

2 × 5ml tsp (2tsp) turmeric

1 green pepper, deseeded and
  cut into strips

1 red pepper, deseeded and cut
  into strips

425ml (¾pt) boiling chicken
  stock, approximately

salt and freshly ground black
  pepper

100g (4oz) frozen peas, thawed

4 tomatoes, skinned, quartered
  and seeds removed

350g (12oz) peeled scampi

225g (8oz) frozen mussels,
  thawed

2 × 15ml tbsp (2tbsp) olive oil

2 shallots, finely chopped

2 cloves garlic, crushed

1 glass dry white wine

275ml (½pt) boiling fish stock
  (page 113)

salt and freshly ground black
  pepper

pinch each cayenne pepper and
  saffron

1 bouquet garni

900g (2lb) mixed white fish,
  skinned and cut into 2.5cm
  (2in) pieces

2 × 5ml tsp (2tsp) cornflour

4 × 15ml tbsp (4tbsp) double
  cream

Paella (*serves 6*)   *colour opposite*
POWER LEVEL: 100% (FULL)

1 Weigh the chicken joints and place in a large casserole dish. Cover and cook, allowing 7–8 min per ½kg (1lb). Turn the dish or rearrange the chicken joints halfway through if necessary. Drain off and reserve the juices. Put the chicken to one side.

2 Place the oil, onion and garlic in the dish, cover and cook for 4 min. Add the rice and turmeric and mix together well. Stir in half the peppers, boiling stock, seasoning and the reserved juices from the chicken. Cover and cook for 10 min, stirring well twice throughout.

3 Stir in the peas and tomatoes and continue to cook for 5 min. Allow to stand for 5 min.

4 Place the remaining pepper strips in a small bowl, cover and cook for 2–3 min, then drain.

5 Remove the skin from the chicken pieces. Add the chicken to the rice with the scampi and mussels, stirring in a little more stock or water if necessary. Cover and cook for 5–6 min until heated through and the scampi are cooked.

6 Arrange the pepper strips over the top of the paella and sprinkle with paprika. Cover and allow to stand for 5 min before serving.

DO NOT FREEZE

For garnish: paprika

Fish provençale (*serves 6*)
POWER LEVEL: 100% (FULL)

1 Place the oil and shallots in a casserole dish, cover and cook for 3 min. Stir in the garlic and wine. Cook, uncovered, for about 4 min until the liquid quantity is reduced by half.

2 Stir in the stock, salt, black pepper, cayenne and saffron. Add the bouquet garni and the fish.

3 Cover and cook for approximately 7 min until the fish is tender. Remove the fish and keep hot. Boil the liquid in the microwave for 5 min until reduced in quantity.

4 Blend the cornflour with a little of the liquid and add to the casserole. Cook for 1–2 min until thickened, stirring once throughout. Remove the bouquet garni and stir in the cream.

5 Return the fish to the sauce and garnish with mussels. Serve hot with warm garlic bread.

For garnish: few cooked mussels in shells
For serving: warm garlic bread (page 114)

Paella (above);
Sole Andalouse (page 84)

Sauces and miscellaneous recipes

Included in this section are recipes for hot and cold sauces and some vegetables, plus basic information and recipe notes which are referred to in various sections throughout the book.

1 egg or 2 egg yolks
2 × 15ml tbsp (2tbsp) white
   vinegar or lemon juice
½ × 5ml tsp (½tsp) salt
¼ × 5ml tsp (¼tsp) each dry
   mustard and pepper
½ × 5ml tsp (½tsp) sugar
150ml (¼pt) salad oil

Blender mayonnaise *(makes about 150ml/¼pt)*

1 Place all the ingredients except the oil in a blender or food processor and blend on maximum speed for 1 min.
2 Gradually add the oil in a steady stream through the lid while the blender or food processor is running.
3 Store in the refrigerator.

DO NOT FREEZE

3–5 cloves garlic, peeled
salt and pepper
1 whole egg and 1 egg yolk *or*
   3 egg yolks
few drops lemon juice
200ml (7½ fl oz) olive oil,
   approximately

Aïoli *(makes about 200ml/⅓pt)*

Aïoli is a very thick mayonnaise sauce with garlic, and this recipe is made quickly in a blender or liquidiser

1 Place all the ingredients except the olive oil into a blender or liquidiser goblet. Blend for 1 min, then gradually pour in the olive oil while the blender is running. Add sufficient oil until the mixture is really thick.
2 Turn out into a bowl or dish and stir well before serving. Serve with fish, chicken, boiled or raw vegetables.

DO NOT FREEZE

To skin tomatoes
POWER LEVEL: 100% (FULL)

1 Pierce the skins of the tomatoes with a sharp knife and place 3–4 at a time in the microwave cooker and heat for 1½–2½ min. Turn them over halfway through.
2 The skins should peel off easily, but the ripeness of the tomatoes will affect the time required. If not quite ready, heat for another ½–1min.

150ml (¼pt) soured cream
2 × 5ml tsp (2tsp) lemon juice
1 × 5ml tsp (1tsp) french
   mustard or horseradish
pinch each salt and sugar, to
   taste

Creamy mustard sauce *(serves 6)*

The sauce goes well with all smoked fish but may also be served with fresh trout or mackerel; horseradish can be used instead of mustard

Mix the soured cream, lemon juice and mustard together and add the salt and sugar to taste. Mix well and serve with fish.

DO NOT FREEZE

Hollandaise sauce *(serves 4)*
POWER LEVEL: 50% (DEFROST)

100g (4oz) butter
2 × 15ml tbsp (2tbsp) wine
   vinegar
2 egg yolks
salt and pepper

1 Melt the butter for 2 min, add the vinegar and egg yolks and whisk lightly.
2 Cook for 1 min, whisk well, season to taste and serve immediately.

DO NOT FREEZE

Vinaigrette dressing

Blend the oil, vinegar, mustard and seasoning by whisking together in a bowl or placing in a screw-top jar and shaking vigorously. Alternatively, blend in a liquidiser. Beat in the chopped herbs if used.

DO NOT FREEZE

150ml (¼pt) oil
3 × 15ml tbsp (3tbsp) wine
   vinegar
½ × 5ml tsp (½tsp) dry
   mustard
salt and freshly ground black
   pepper
1 × 15ml tbsp (1tbsp) chopped
   fresh herbs (optional)

French dressing

Follow the ingredients and method for vinaigrette dressing, omitting the herbs.

DO NOT FREEZE

White sauce *(makes about 275ml/½pt)*
POWER LEVEL: 100% (FULL)

25g (1oz) butter
25g (1oz) plain flour
275ml (½pt) milk
salt and pepper

1 Melt the butter in a medium-sized glass bowl for 1–1½ min. Blend in the flour and gradually stir in the milk.
2 Add the seasoning and cook for 4–5 min, stirring every minute. Use as required.

Variations

One of the following ingredients may be added to the sauce 2 min before the end of the cooking time:

Prawn sauce: 100g (4oz) peeled prawns
Cheese sauce: 50–75g (2–3oz) cheese, grated
Mushroom sauce: 50g (2oz) mushrooms, chopped
Onion sauce: 100g (4oz) cooked onion, chopped
Parsley sauce: 2 × 5ml tsp (2tsp) parsley, chopped
Egg sauce: 1 hard-boiled egg, chopped finely

White wine sauce

Follow the recipe for white sauce, substituting a wine glass of dry white wine for the same measure of milk.

Velouté sauce

Follow the recipe for white sauce, replacing the milk with the same quantity of light chicken or fish stock. When cooked, stir in 2 × 15ml tbsp (2tbsp) double cream.

225g (8oz) gooseberries, topped and tailed
90ml (3fl oz) water
1–2 × 15ml tbsp (1–2tbsp) caster sugar
25g (1oz) butter
1 × 15ml tbsp (1tbsp) chopped fennel *or* 1 × 5ml tsp (1tsp) ground fennel (optional)

1 medium head fennel, washed and trimmed
2 × 15ml tbsp (2tbsp) salted water
15g (½oz) butter
15g (½oz) flour
salt and pepper
275ml (½pt) milk and fennel juice, mixed
3 × 15ml tbsp (3tbsp) single cream

Gooseberry sauce *(makes about 275ml/½pt)*
POWER LEVEL: 100% (FULL)

This sauce is traditionally served with stuffed mackerel, but without the chopped fennel it goes very well with smoked mackerel instead of the more usual horseradish sauce, and may also be served with cold turkey or chicken

1 Place all the ingredients in a covered bowl or dish.
2 Cook for 3–4 min, shaking or stirring halfway through, or until the gooseberries pop open.

Fennel sauce *(serves 4)*
POWER LEVEL: 100% (FULL)

This sauce makes a good accompaniment to salmon or mackerel

1 Cut the fennel into small pieces and cook with the salted water in a covered dish or boiling bag for 6–7 min. Drain off the juices and reserve.
2 Chop the fennel finely.
3 Melt the butter. add the flour and seasonings. Make the reserved juices up to 275ml (½pt) with milk and add gradually to the roux, stirring continously. Stir in the fennel. (If preferred, the sauce may be puréed in a blender or food processor at this stage.)
4 Heat the sauce for 4–5 min until thickened and bubbling, stirring every 30 sec.
5 Allow the sauce to cool slightly and stir in the cream. Serve hot with fish.

Salmon Steaks with Fennel Sauce (page 70)

1 small onion
6 cloves
1 bay leaf
6 peppercorns
1 blade mace
275ml (½pt) milk
25g (1oz) butter
25g (1oz) flour
salt and pepper

Béchamel sauce *(makes about 275ml/½pt)*
POWER LEVEL: 100% (FULL) OR 50% (DEFROST)

1 Peel the onion and stick with the cloves. Place in a bowl with the rest of the spices and milk.
2 Heat without boiling. Cook for 3 min, stand for 3 min; heat for 2 min, stand for 3 min. Alternatively, heat on 50% (defrost) setting for 10–11 min. This allows the infusion of the flavours from the spices into the milk.
3 Melt the butter for 1 min and stir in the flour and seasonings. Strain the milk and add a little at a time to the butter and flour mixture (the roux), stirring continuously.
4 Cook for 1½–2 min, stirring every ½ min until thickened and bubbling. Adjust seasoning if necessary.

1 × 15ml tbsp (1tbsp) olive oil
1 large onion, peeled and finely chopped
1–2 cloves garlic, crushed or finely chopped
397g (14oz) can tomatoes, drained
1 × 15ml tbsp (1tbsp) tomato purée
1 glass red wine or juice from tomatoes
few sprigs fresh herbs *or*
1 × 5ml tsp (1tsp) dried herbs, eg thyme or rosemary
salt and freshly ground black pepper

Tomato sauce *(makes about 275ml/½pt)*
POWER LEVEL: 100% (FULL)

1 Place the olive oil, onion and garlic in a bowl and toss well. Cover and cook for 4–5 min until soft.
2 Roughly chop the tomatoes and add to the bowl with the remaining ingredients.
3 Cook, uncovered, until soft and the liquid quantity is reduced, giving a fairly thick sauce. Stir every 3 min.
4 Use when referred to in recipes or where a well-flavoured tomato sauce is required.

100g (4oz) butter
1–2 × 15ml tbsp (1–2tbsp) finely chopped parsley
salt and freshly ground black pepper
few drops lemon juice

Parsley butter

Savoury butters can be quickly made and used to ring the changes with plainly cooked fish fillets or steaks

Blend the butter and parsley together. Season to taste with a little salt and black pepper and a few drops of lemon juice. Chill slightly before serving.

Variations

Alternative savoury butters can be made using the above recipe, but substituting one of the following ingredients for the parsley.

Anchovy: 6 anchovy fillets, washed, dried, pounded or sieved, *or* 1–2 × 5ml tsp (1–2tsp) anchovy paste
Crab: 100g (4oz) crabmeat, pounded
Shrimp: 100g (4oz) peeled shrimps, pounded or blended
Lemon: 1 lemon, grated rind
Tomato: 2 × 15ml tbsp (2tbsp) tomato purée
Mushroom: 100g (4oz) mushrooms, cooked, pounded or blended
Garlic: 1–4 cloves garlic, crushed

Fish stock *(makes about 550ml/1pt)*
POWER LEVEL: 100% (FULL) AND 30%

Use the trimmings of the fish, such as bones, head and the skin, to make this fish stock. Almost any white fish can be used, but as it does not keep well the stock should be used preferably on the day it is made

1   Place the fish trimmings in a large bowl or jug with the water and a little salt. Cover and bring to the boil in the microwave. Remove the bowl and take off any scum from the surface of the water.
2   Add the onion, celery and bouquet garni, cover and cook on 30% setting for 30 min.
3   Strain the stock through a sieve or a fine cloth. Store in the refrigerator until required.

450g (1lb) fish trimmings, washed well
550ml (1pt) water
salt
1 onion, finely chopped
1 stick celery, finely chopped
bouquet garni

Buttered cucumber *(serves 4)*
POWER LEVEL: 100% (FULL)

1   Wash the cucumber, trim off the ends and discard. Peel the cucumber if preferred and cut the flesh into dice. Place into a boiling bag, roasting bag or covered casserole dish.
2   Sprinkle with salt to taste and toss well. Add the butter and cook for 3½–4½ min, shaking or tossing well halfway through. Take care not to overcook as the cucumber should remain crispy.
3   Drain before serving hot, garnished with chopped parsley, dill or mint.

DO NOT FREEZE

For garnish: chopped parsley, dill or mint (optional)

450g (1lb) cucumber
salt for sprinkling
25g (1oz) butter

Creamed potatoes *(serves 4)*
POWER LEVEL: 100% (FULL)

1   Prick the skins of the potatoes with a fork. Place with the salted water in a casserole dish, cover and cook for 10–12 min until tender. Test with a fork.
2   Drain the potatoes, remove the skins or cut in half and scoop out the potato from the skins.
3   Mash the potatoes with a fork or potato masher. If required for piping through a forcing bag and nozzle, it will be necessary to sieve or purée them in a blender or food processor.
4   Heat the milk for 1 min and add to the potatoes with the butter and seasoning. Beat together well and serve hot.

450g (1lb) potatoes, washed
2 × 15ml tbsp (2tbsp) salted water
90–100ml (3–4fl oz) milk
25g (1oz) butter
salt and pepper

Braised celery *(serves 4)*
POWER LEVEL: 100% (FULL)

1   Melt the butter for 1 min in a shallow dish. Trim the rind from the rashers and cut them into strips.
2   Add the bacon strips and onion to the butter, toss well, cover and cook for 2 min. Add the celery and cook for a further 2 min.
3   Pour on the stock, add the seasoning, cover and cook for 15–20 min. Serve hot.

25g (1oz) butter
2 rashers bacon
1 small onion, peeled and finely chopped
350g (12oz) celery, cut into 7.5cm (3in) strips
275ml (½pt) boiling chicken stock
salt and pepper

450g (1lb) button onions or
    shallots
boiling water
25g (1oz) butter
2 × 5ml tsp (2tsp) caster sugar

Glazed onions (*serves 4–5*)
POWER LEVEL: 100% (FULL)

1 Peel the onions and place in a large bowl or casserole dish. Pour on sufficient boiling water to cover.
2 Cover the dish and bring the water to the boil in the microwave. Drain off the water from the onions.
3 Add the butter to the onions, cover and cook for 5 min. Shake the dish to stir the onions and sprinkle with the caster sugar.
4 Cook, uncovered, for 3–4 min until tender and glazed. Serve hot.

40g (1½oz) butter
1 small onion, chopped
1 small stick celery, chopped
225g (8oz) long grain rice
pinch saffron (optional)
boiling water
425ml (¾pt) boiling chicken
    stock, approximately
salt and pepper
50–75g (2–3oz) currants
    (optional)
50–75g (2–3oz) pistachio nuts
    or almonds, blanched and
    shredded (optional)

Rice pilaf (*serves 4*)
POWER LEVEL: 100% (FULL)

1 Melt the butter in a large shallow dish for 2 min. Add the onion and celery and cook for 3 min. Stir in the rice and cook for 1 min.
2 Soak the saffron in 2 × 15ml (2tbsp) boiling water. Mix together the stock, saffron and seasoning and cook, uncovered, for 12–15min, adding extra stock if necessary.
3 Carefully stir in the currants and nuts if used, and fork over the pilaf before serving.

225g (8oz) long grain,
    easy-cook rice
550ml (1pt) boiling salted water
1 × 15ml tbsp (1tbsp) oil

Boiled rice (*serves 4–6*)
POWER LEVEL: 100% (FULL)

1 Place the rice in a large bowl and add the boiling salted water and oil.
2 Cover and cook for 10–12 min, allow to stand for 5 min. Drain and rinse under hot water if necessary before serving.

225g (8oz) egg noodles or
    tagliatelle
550ml (1pt) boiling salted water
1 × 15ml tbsp (1tbsp) oil

Noodles (*serves 2–3*)
POWER LEVEL: 100% (FULL)

1 Place the noodles in a large bowl, add boiling salted water to cover and the oil. Stir well.
2 Cover and bring to the boil in the microwave, then cook for 4–5 min. Allow to stand for 2 min. Drain and serve.

1 short crusty french stick
150g (5oz) butter, softened
3–4 cloves garlic, crushed or
    finely chopped *or* 1–1½ ×
    5ml tsp (1–1½tsp) garlic
    powder

Garlic bread (*1 loaf*)
POWER LEVEL: 100% (FULL)

Delicious as a snack or accompaniment to a meal

1 Cut the loaf, not quite through, into slices 2.5cm (1in) thick.
2 Cream the butter and beat in the garlic. Spread large knobs of butter between the slices.
3 Protect the thin ends of the loaf with small smooth pieces of aluminium foil. Place on kitchen paper in the microwave cooker and cover with a piece of damp kitchen paper.
4 Cook for 1½ min or until the butter has just melted and the bread is warmed through.

Fish Korma (page 21);
Prawn Curry (page 63)

Herb bread

Follow the ingredients and method for garlic bread, but substituting 1 × 15ml tbsp (1tbsp) finely chopped fresh mixed herbs or 2 × 5ml tsp (2tsp) dried mixed herbs for the garlic.

Pizza dough (*makes 3 large or 4 small pizzas*)
POWER LEVEL: 100% (FULL)

1 × 5ml tsp (1tsp) sugar
275ml (½pt) water,
   approximately
2 × 5ml tsp (2tsp) dried yeast
450g (1lb) plain flour
1½ × 5ml tsp (1½tsp) salt
3 × 15ml tbsp (3tbsp) olive oil

1 Lightly grease 3–4 × 20–25cm (8–10in) plates.
2 Add the sugar to half the water and heat for 30 sec. Stir in the yeast and leave to activate.
3 Sift the flour and salt and warm for 30 sec. Warm the rest of the water for 30 sec.
4 Add the yeast mixture to the flour and mix to a soft dough with the rest of the water, adjusting the quantity if necessary. When the mixture is smooth, turn onto a floured surface and knead well.
5 Place the dough in a bowl, cover with clingfilm and prove by heating for 15 sec, then letting it rest for 5–10 min. Repeat 3–4 times until dough is double in size.
6 Knead the dough again, this time working in the oil, a little at a time, until all the oil is absorbed and the dough is pliable and smooth.
7 Shape the dough by rolling or pressing into 3 larger or 4 smaller rounds to fit the prepared plates. Prove each round separately in rotation in the microwave as described above until well risen.

Shortcrust pastry (*for a 20cm/8in flan case*)
POWER LEVEL: 100% (FULL)

175g (6oz) plain flour, or plain
   and wholemeal mixed
pinch salt
75g (3oz) butter or margarine
2 × 5ml tsp (2tsp) caster sugar
   (optional)
1 egg yolk
2 × 15ml tbsp (2tbsp) water

1 Sift the flour with the salt and rub in the butter or margarine until the mixture resembles fine crumbs. Stir in the sugar if used.
2 Beat the egg yolk with the water and add the flour. Mix together well, then knead lightly.
3 Chill before rolling out.

To line a flan dish

Roll out the pastry into a circle 5cm (2in) larger than the dish. Wrap the pastry loosely around the rolling pin and lift into the flan dish. Ease the pastry into shape, removing any air from under the base, pressing well into the sides and taking care not to stretch the pastry. Cut the pastry away, but leave 6mm (¼in) above the rim of the flan dish. Carefully ease this down into the dish, or flute the edges and leave slightly higher than the rim of the dish (this allows a little extra height to the sides of the flan case to allow for any shrinkage during cooking). Alternatively, roll the rolling pin across the top of the flan dish to cut off surplus pastry. Prick the base well with a fork.

To bake blind

Using a long smooth strip of aluminium foil measuring approximately 3.75cm (1½in) wide, line the inside, upright edge of the pastry flan case. This protects the edges from overcooking in the microwave. Place two pieces of absorbent kitchen paper over the base, easing around the edges and pressing gently into the corners to help to keep the foil strip in position. Place in the microwave and cook for 4–4½ min, giving the dish a quarter turn every minute. Remove the kitchen paper and foil and cook for a further 1–2 min.

Alternative conventional bake

Line the pastry flan case with a circle of lightly greased greaseproof paper (greased side down) or kitchen paper. Half fill the paper with uncooked beans, lentils, small pasta or rice which may be specially kept for this purpose. Alternatively, line the pastry flan case with foil only. Cook in a pre-heated oven at 200°C (400°F) Mark 6 for 15–20 min, until the pastry is nearly cooked. Remove lining and bake for 5–10 min until the base is firm and dry.

Pancakes

100g (4oz) plain flour
pinch salt
1 egg, beaten
275ml (½pt) milk
oil for frying

Pancakes cannot be cooked successfully in the microwave, so are best cooked conventionally; this basic pancake batter is sufficient to make 8–10 thin pancakes

1 Sift the flour and salt into a mixing bowl. Make a well in the centre and drop in the beaten egg.
2 Slowly pour on half the milk, mixing the egg and milk into the flour with a wooden spoon.
3 Beat the mixture with a wooden spoon or whisk until smooth and free of lumps.
4 Add the remaining milk, whisking continuously until the mixture is bubbly and the consistency of single cream.
5 Heat a 17.5–20cm (7–8in) frying pan on a conventional hotplate or burner. Just sufficient oil should be added to prevent the pancakes from sticking.
6 The pan and oil should be really hot. Pour in just enough batter to allow a thin film to coat the base of the pan, tilting the pan to spread the mixture.
7 The base of the pancake should be cooked in about 1 min. Flip the pancake over with a palette knife or spatula and cook the other side for about 1 min. If the pancakes are taking too long to cook, adjust the heat or make sure that too much batter is not being used.
8 Layer the pancakes in absorbent kitchen paper and keep warm if to be used immediately. Alternatively, leave to cool, or freeze as they may be thawed and reheated most satisfactorily in the microwave.
9 Fill and use as required, allowing one per person if served as a starter to a meal or two if served as a snack or as a main course with vegetables.

Note: *The ingredients for the pancake batter may be blended in a liquidiser or food processor*

Index

Numbers in italics refer to illustrations